RED IVY TEA

H. David Boyles, Jr

Contents

Dedication i

Acknowledgments ii

About the Author iii

Introduction 1

Chapter One New Resident Harry Campo There's No Place Like Home 2

Chapter Two Old Resident: Evan Springfield Some Day The Kid's Will Thank Us 8

Chapter Three Old Resident: Billy Hugh Cooper With Tribute To Miss Eva 15

Chapter Four Old Resident Ellis Hienkle, Give Me That Old Time Religion 20

Chapter Five Old Resident: Bud Jackson and His Infamous Finger 27

Chapter Six Builder Supervisor Allen Staton Springfield Estates Groundbreaking 30

Chapter Seven Springfield Estates Homecoming 36

Chapter Eight Springfield Estates If Only There Was A McDonald's Nearby 40

Chapter Nine Soon To Be New Resident Jack Owens and His Daughter Kelly 43

Chapter Ten Jack's Wife Patty What Channel Are You Watching? 52

Chapter Eleven Ode to All the Harrys' in the World 60

Chapter Twelve Harry's Moving Day 66

Chapter Thirteen The Accident Miracles Come In Many Shapes and Sizes 69

Chapter Fourteen Harry Helps Build A Barn What A Wise Guy 82

Chapter Fifteen Old Resident: Ellis Heinkle's Wife Clara, Rn Rural Nurse 92

Chapter Sixteen New Resident Will Ziefer Friend of Wernher Von Braun 108

Chapter Seventeen Saturday Afternoon in Paradise. Where Is Burt Reynolds When You Need Him? 113

Chapter Eighteen Neighbor Helping Neighbor What Would the World Do Without Harry 120

Chapter Nineteen Patty's Grandpa - Beyond the Sunset 125

Dedication

I dedicate this book to Clyde W Cox and Edward L Dellinger. Both of these men had a tremendous influence on me and believed in me at a time in my life when I didn't even believe in myself. I will always be grateful to you both.

Acknowledgments

I want to acknowledge my parents, Hubert David Sr. and Maggie Amanda Boyles, two of the finest people that ever walked this planet.

Dad, I am sure there were times you regretted naming me after you. And Mom, I remember the times when food was scarce that you 'just really weren't hungry'. I will never forget when it dawned on me what you were doing. I absolutely adore you both.

About the Author

Born in Springfield, Missouri, and raised as the eldest son of a Pentecostal preacher, H. David Boyles, Jr. has cultivated a diverse perspective through a career in international sales, spanning 40 countries.

Now retired, Boyles channels his worldly experiences into his passions: writing, music, and fostering meaningful connections with audiences.

In his debut novel "RED IVY TEA", Boyles invites readers on a captivating voyage to 1975 Springfield, North Carolina. Through vivid characters and masterful storytelling, he delves into themes of tradition, progress, and identity with profound insight.

Additionally, his recent album release, "Songs From Life's Mostly Good Ride", offers a soul-stirring musical experience, showcasing his artistic versatility. Available now on Spotify.

Married for three decades, to Karen I Boyles. H. David Boyles, Jr. dedication to his craft and his ability to touch hearts through both literature and music make him a truly multifaceted artist, resonating deeply with audiences and inviting them on a journey of discovery and reflection.

Introduction

The year is 1975 in the sleepy small town of Springfield, North Carolina. Very little has changed there over the decades, and the townsfolk were perfectly content to keep it that way. A developer bought a sizable tract of vacant land there and created a development consisting of upscale single-family homes. Suffice it to say, the locals were not at all pleased. Things would never be the same for either the old or the new residents of the town of Springfield. This novella series describes some of those good and bad changes that these new neighbors shared and endured. I hope you enjoy their story.

Chapter One
New Resident Harry Campo
There's No Place Like Home

Where pray tell is the tranquility? The serenity? That overall feeling of satisfaction from living in peace and harmony with nature and man? I'll never trust another real estate agent as long as I live, Harry swore as he gazed out the window of his new home in Springfield Estates Rural Paradise.

Harry always got reflective when he was upset with himself. No man could dodge the truth more effectively or present a misconception more convincingly. The house on a one-acre lot that he had bought from Gleason Builders was a bargain and a damn good one at that. One full acre. That worked out to 43,560 square feet. That was half a city block back home or close to it, and he owned it all.

Along with twenty-seven pines, three white oaks, two tulip poplars and one bush with red berries that no one had ever seen before and couldn't identify. Not even the tobacco-chewing Buncombe County agricultural agent that Harry had called because he felt he would know about such things. Harry was sorry that he had called as soon as the agent got out of his truck. For one thing, he had a scruffy, unkempt beard; for another, he was huge. Damn, all men up here looked like amazons. All the women, too, for that matter. And none of them knew how to smile, at least not at him. Harry had hoped that this county man would look like that friendly little county agent Hank Kimball on the old television show 'Green Acres' for some reason. Not to be.

As it turned out, the county man didn't know what the mysterious red-berried bush was either. In fact, he looked absolutely put out for having been called out such a long way for such a menial task. He glared at Harry as they stood around the bush and silently moved the tobacco juice from one side of his mouth to the other as if considering whether to discharge the contents onto the bush or onto Harry.

Harry got a little nervous as he realized that the agent was probably leaning in favor of the bush. "So, this is what you called me all the way from Asheville, this one little fart of a bush? May I ask you what it is about this bush worth me driving seventy-eight miles to look at?"

Harry's heart started beating double time, and he was afraid he would get sick. But he took a deep breath and stood his ground. "Well, Mr. Delmar, you did say your last name was Delmar, didn't you, Mr. Delmar? I'm relatively new to the area and haven't had a real opportunity to study the various species of plants that are indigenous to the area, but according to everyone that I have had a chance to discuss this particular bush with, all are in agreement that they have never seen anything remotely like it before. Therefore, in my assumption that I may have a relatively rare find here thought it only benefitting to contact the proper agencies to confirm what I and many others in the area, I assure you, feel may be a true botanical find." He exhaled.

The county man didn't say a word for two solid minutes; he just looked straight at Harry without moving a muscle. Not even his jaw, which soon filled to overflowing with tobacco juice. He finally slowly looked from Harry to the now insignificant bush and spat right down into the middle of it, knocking off at least six berries in the process. He used his thumb and forefinger to wipe off the corners of his mouth and rubbed them vigorously together. Then he smiled.

"Mr. Campo, you did say that your last name was Campo, didn't you? Yes, Mr. Campo, we at the Buncombe County Agricultural Department appreciate your feeling of civic duty by informing us of this rare red-berried bush. And I want to assure you that as soon as I get back to the office, I will put my entire staff onto this case and see if we have something worthy of the Smithsonian. Now, you just water this thing every day and make sure it gets plenty of natural sunlight and very shortly, I'll return with a few crack specialists to see what we can make of this. Who knows, maybe they'll name this thing after you; you'll become immortal.

Harry was being conned, and he knew it. He wanted to cry and was afraid he would; therefore, he kept his mouth shut. The county man couldn't resist one last barb. "Yes, sir; maybe they'll name this thing after you. Maybe, the 'Campo Bush', no better yet, the 'Harry Bush'. The county man couldn't contain himself anymore thinking about that and just exploded into laughter. The sounds of the man's laughter were still burning in Harry's ears as he watched the truck drive out of sight.

Harry was so emotionally overcome that he just stood there and shook nervously, with some of his facial muscles twisting spasmodically. How could anyone be so cruel, so heartless, so unfeeling to other people? What did he ever do to that man to make him treat him like that? All people could hurt Harry easily, and all people did. Children, old men, young women, car wash attendants, blue collar, white collar, men of the collar, all were hell-bent on unleashing as much hurt on him as he could possibly stand. So, he usually kept to himself.

Actually, most people liked Harry in a very distant sort of way and felt that a little psychiatric help would do him a world of good. His kid sister had mentioned this to him once in a show of genuine compassion, hoping he would realize whatever social oversight he had missed out on in the growing process. She mentioned that to him on February 17, 1971, the last time that the two of them had spoken.

Sherry's revelation was one of the cruelest blows that Harry had experienced in his entire life. He knew that the world was evil and conniving. But he always felt that his family would stand there with him.

Not that they ever showed it. But still, they were church-going people who loved God and his ways. And the Bible did say something about family loving family, of that he was certain. 'Honor thy father and mother and the rest, and ye shall see God.' Excuviticus 3: something or Leukemia 44:9. Somewhere around there. So when his baby sister attacked him, the pain was deep-seated. He had let his guard down to a family member and she had sensed it. Harry wondered when his sister had crossed over. How had the devil gained control of her thoughts? Sherry used to be so nice, never making fun of him or anything like all the others did. But she was weak. He knew what Sherry would do now that she had succeeded in reducing his manhood; he had seen it so often by so many others. Come back friendly as if nothing was ever said and try to get him to lower his guard again. Yet, no one ever came back to say they were sorry for the irreparable damage that they had done to what was left of his heart.

The God/devil fight was raging all around him, and God was losing! Everybody was crossing over. Terrible works, terrible actions, terrible thoughts and all of them were directed at Harry, the last great holdout for decency, morality, prayer in schools, segregation and sexual abstinence, a problem that existed for Harry and bothered him often. He wasn't married. If there was just one good woman in the world, he would have, but nay, not one.

Women were confusing creatures who were ruled by their emotions, passed blood once a month and gave Adam the apple in the garden that started all of this mess in the first place. How could God, with his infinitesimal wisdom, not have realized what he was doing when he created a being that was ruled by their emotions? Imagine!

Harry sometimes got downright emotional thinking about it. No other creature on the face of this earth was relegated to by their emotions like women were. And it was a good thing that they were not, or else there would be no other creature on the face of this earth. Harry always figured that man's great intellect was the only thing that saved him from losing himself to women's emotional whims. The whole world survived on man's ability to think. Such things bothered Harry frequently and made him wish for younger days of happier thoughts that he never had and better times that he never knew.

Chapter Two
Old Resident: Evan Springfield
Some Day The Kid's Will Thank Us

Evan Springfield was a hardworking man whose family had lived in Springfield as far back as anyone could remember. They were good, hard-working people who had worked their 263 acres with the help of their four children, a small family by community standards.

Children were an asset, no matter how you looked at it. Tax write-offs; even country folk knew about that and had to pay taxes. But more importantly, kids were unhired hands and bodies to work gardens, tend cattle, fix barn roofs, overhaul tractors and run fence lines.

They were also dear souls to be loved with all of their parents' hearts. Hard work came early to kids, values were instilled young and very few knew the meaning of bad nerves. Country living provided its generic brand of tranquilizer, namely, hard work. Tired kids usually didn't have the desire to booze it up all night when sleep was far more enticing.

Bending to pick beans, pull corn or pull up potatoes made bellies harder than any Nautilus machine ever could. Loading a barn with freshly cut hay would build biceps and pecs far more effectively than any universal machine and wouldn't cost nearly as much.

The slaughtering of pigs, cows, rabbits, squirrels, chickens or any type of canning or freezer stock was usually a family affair, from the initial killing to the final cutting and cleaning. Of course, it was a shock at first, but it soon instilled the understanding into their young minds that for them to live, some animals may have to die. Kids learned to cope with the unpleasant aspects of life early on, which helped them establish an order of priorities, beginning with the very basics. They grew up constantly learning with life being the class teacher; their formal education was a secondary influence in the learning process.

Real education came in self-sufficiency taught by repairing motors, building barns and sheds, wiring houses, laying drain lines, growing their own food, filling their own freezer, canning their own vegetables, yet living at peace with their neighbors and usually their own kin.

Learning by doing. To country folks, it was a far better motto that made far more sense than learning by textbook. And what, then, did college really teach anybody? College instilled the opinion that a four-year piece of paper was more important than knowing how to build a house and a six-year piece of paper more important than knowing how to survive a depression.

Evan knew all of these things and had raised his kids to live by this unwritten code. But the world was changing and changing rapidly. Children were forced to go to school through the twelfth grade now and the system of education had become standardized by the federal government. Teachers had to be college-educated, so naturally, a college education was shown in a favorable light in the classroom. In fairness, it did open the minds of country kids, making them realize that there was a very big world out there and they were limiting theirs' to an approximately fifty mile radius from home. More and more time from work was spent in retrospection or daydreaming, as it was better known by those who knew.

"What the hell difference does it make? What made the cloud, boy? Evan argued with his oldest son, Jasper. "Come on, Daddy, haven't you ever wondered why that cloud is fluffy like a ball of cotton today when tomorrow it might come in dark, low and full of lightning?"

"No, son, I have never wondered about that because there ain't a damn thing l can do to change it. If them meteorologists think that they can change it, then I let them think about it, though I'd bet your mama's life that they couldn't change a light bulb. Son, some things you've got to let God and nature take care of. Everything is done to a plan and a purpose, and today the plan is for there to be big fluffy clouds in the sky. Boy, you are getting to where you are cluttering your mind with shit. Some things are God's business, so just leave it at that."

But he knew that Jasper would not just leave it at that now or ever again. And he was right. More and more, Jasper became more insightful, more sensitive, more introspective, more in quest of truths that could never be tested, facts that could never be proven, solutions that could never be attained. In other words, Jasper became a dope. Introspection became more important than happiness, and fashion took the place of comfort; a sixth sense overruled common sense.

High school arrived far too quickly and left just as suddenly, and Jasper wanted college. Evan was afraid of the thought of it but at the same time, he knew it was inevitable. He had known it for at least three years. Wondering where he had gone wrong with the boy would be nothing short of a waste of time. It was far too late for that, and he knew it. Maybe college was the answer. Maybe he would go and get a firsthand look at all of this nonsense that he had been led to believe was true and come back down to earth.

Evan was not having any affect in that area, of that he was sure. Yes, maybe college was the answer. A good technical college, maybe a state school. Engineering. Yea, damn right. He had heard some of the things that those boys could do. Surveying, hell, yes, that would really come in handy, good money too. Civil Engineering, yessiree, Civil Engineering. Those guys could figure out buildings' stresses and draw house plans; banks required those these days.

Evan thought about the plans that he had used when he built his house forty years ago. He'd drawn the layout on a cardboard box top. After forty years, it was still standing with the ridge board as straight as an arrow. And all from a cardboard box top. That's the kind of thing that country teaches you, he thought aloud within earshot of no one. Now, you had to have an eight-page thick set of plans, including elevations, foundations, floor layouts, framing and erecting specs, cabinet plans and bills of materials. All at the whopping cost of 200 dollars! Damn government. Well, if Jasper can learn how to do that, then OK, college would be all right after all. Yessiree. Maybe this will be AOK.

It was not OK two days later when Jasper informed him of his choice of colleges and majors - North Carolina - Philosophy. North Carolina, a preppy school where rich kids went and a major that he'd never heard of.

"Jasper, what in the hell is philosophy?"

"Dad, please call me Jazz; everybody else does and has for years. Nobody even knows me as Jasper anymore. It's embarrassing when you call me that in front of people."

Evan let Jazz's words sink in and then turned crimson. "Boy, I have finally realized what is going on. Finally, after all these years,

I finally see what in the damn hell is going on here. You are ashamed of your own family. All of us. Not just me who has worked like a pack mule to keep you fed, happy and well, but also your mother, brothers and sisters as well. Your poor mother, who changed your shitty diapers when you were a baby, who set up with you many a night when you were too sick to wipe the puke off your own mouth, you are ashamed of her too. And now, Mister High and Mighty, you change the name that we gave you at your birth, the name you had when the preacher dedicated you to God because your newfound friends who couldn't give two shakes of a cat's ass about you think it sounds hip or cool or whatever other damn word that your little group thinks is cute. Well, let me tell you, Jasper, let your cool friends send your jazzy ass off to college because that is the only way that you're going."

"Daddy, I'm not ashamed of you or anybody in this family, nor have I ever been. Jazz is just short for Jasper; that's all. Jasper was strangely calm for reasons that he wasn't even sure of. "I don't want to go to college to rebel against you or to make you ashamed of me. I've just got to learn how to sort out these questions that make my brain want to explode. You understand that, don't you? You always told me to get all the facts upfront and do everything to the best of my ability. Well, that's all I'm doing, just getting the facts together."

Evan was quiet for a long time, and Jazz knew he had won. Damn, he thought to himself, maybe I'll major in psychology.

Jazz was still undecided on his major when he heard the news about his father's death two years later. He was still undecided on his major when they laid Evan to rest at the cemetery at Springfield Baptist Church. He was even undecided when he sold his portion of the farm that Evan had left him to Gleason Builders for $2,000 per acre.

Chapter Three
Old Resident: Billy Hugh Cooper
With Tribute To Miss Eva

The whole community went into deep shock when they heard what Jasper Springfield had done. Billy Hugh was more vocal in his criticism than most but that was because his property directly bordered the Springfield home place. Already the surveyors had busied themselves laying off subdivision property lines, plotting imaginary roads and marking trees that would remain after the dozing started.

Jasper's portion of the old Springfield estate equaled approximately 44.86 acres which was working out to 35 building sites. The thought of 35 families living on such a small parcel of land would have been laughable if it weren't for claw hammers pounding the sobering message into everyone's brains.

Gleason Builders Proudly Presents Springfield Estates

One Acre Tracts Nestled In A Quaint Rural Setting Just 80 Miles From Asheville

Small Town Benefits Without Big City Hassles

Jasper was nowhere to be found. Three days after Evan's funeral, Jazz was back in school which is where everyone in

Springfield prayed that he would stay this time. "Poor Evan; if he only knew. And not even cold in the ground yet, either." Billy Hugh Cooper had a captive audience and decided to capitalize on the opportunity.

He always favored himself as the town orator even if no one else did. All were gathered at Springfield Hardware, a large 100-year-old two-story wooden building with functional window shutters, three chimneys and a ten-foot porch wrapped around three sides of the building. Several of the regulars had gathered there as they had been doing every Saturday morning at 5:30 AM.

No one remembered exactly how these morning meetings started but suffice it to say the meeting became as much a part of the week for the local men as their morning constitutional.

"Poor Evan" Billy Hugh repeated, turning toward the porch railing and clamping his hand on it for added emphasis. "Worked that land for many years, as his father did and his father before him. That land's been in that family for as far back as the tax maps go. And now, just like that, it's no more.

Just because one greedy no good son of an uppity bitch decides that he's too good for his kin and his kind. He lowered his voice a little each time someone came on the porch that the group didn't know. "The question now is what are we going to do about it. I have a few ideas. We could …"

"Billy Hugh, we can talk about this later. Not the place, not the time. Too many unknown people were walking around." Billy Hugh didn't let up. "Look, nothing gets done until someone takes the lead..." Calvin Trexler, a member of the gathered group stood up and practically shouted at him." And you are that man? You Billy Hugh? I will never forget nor will I ever forgive you for talking us into 'taking care' of Miss Eva.

Do you remember her, Billy Hugh? That sweet lady didn't deserve what you conjured up for her." Billy Hugh's face turned red. "Look, you cannot pin that on me. All of you went through 'the yellow dog initiation' just like I did. We all took the same vow.

We all agreed. It's not right that you bring that up after all these years." Billy Hugh exhaled. Calvin raised his hand. "OK, you're right. Just shut up OK?" It's OK. The trouble was that Billy Hugh didn't know how to shut up.

Miss Eva was the social butterfly of Springfield. She taught dance and gave singing lessons to those interested. Always smiling, always singing. Really, just a good-natured soul. Every year around Easter she would host the Springfield Beauty Pageant for the local girls. There was never a swimsuit competition; it didn't seem proper but nobody cared. The winners were given a bouquet of flowers and a trophy. In truth, everyone enjoyed themselves.

Then, in 1961, Miss Eva started planning the event and announced the contestants for the upcoming contest. And #4 was Ella McPhail. A true beauty, possibly the prettiest girl in the county. No one challenged that opinion because it was obvious. A rare beauty.

One problem, Ella McPhail was black. Light-skinned maybe but still black. The contest was for white girls and always had been, and Miss Eva damn well knew that. Several approached her quietly and explained what she obviously was not seeing. She just smiled and told them things were changing and we had to change with the times.

No amount of talking could dissuade her and the show did go on. It was a grand affair. Balloons, colorful crepe paper, red carpet. Talent was good, consisting mostly of off-key singers. Contestant #4 was the exception. Her voice was as pretty as she was. When all had finished their routines and explained how they were going to change the world, the results were announced.

The winner was obvious to all in attendance…..Sally Newsome; petite redhead Sally Newsome. Ella McPhail came in dead last. Miss Eva was beaming, just so proud of her pageant. She talked to her husband non-stop all the way home.

When they got in bed, she had a hard time sleeping. It really did go well. Later in the night, they were awakened by a crackling sound from out in the yard along with a flickering bright light.

What the hell was that? They went out onto the covered entry to see the prettiest burning cross bound up in soaked kerosene rags right out in their front yard. The color drained from her face as she realized what was happening. This was a message. No harm done, no foul. Just a warning.

She closed the front door as her husband went out the side entry to douse the flames and tear down the cross. He showered and they went back to bed. Neither said a word or slept a wink all night.

From that day forward Eva was a changed woman. The sweet smile and quick-to-laugh demeanor never returned. She closed her studio and tended to stay home most of the time. Not one soul ever mentioned the cross to her. Ever.

Chapter Four
Old Resident Ellis Hienkle,
Give Me That Old Time Religion

Ellis Hershal Hienkle

Clara Elaine Hienkle

Born: June 18, 1915

Born: September 28, 1919

Died: ?

Died: ?

The only living couple in Springfield that was totally prepared for their death. There were very few people who believed that Ellis would actually buy the tombstone but in Ellis' mind, there was never any doubt. The price was just too 'rock bottom.' Besides, he was really doing it for the children that he loved.

He knew that someday and maybe someday soon, his estate would have to buy him one, so why not save them money on what would be a most grievous chore for them to carry out.

Ellis had no way of knowing at the time that he would live another thirty years and be buried under a stone so covered in moss that one could barely make out his name. It was sad for everyone when the deal turned out to be for the benefit of Clara.

So there it stood, proudly on the tenth row from the side entrance of the cemetery; the tomb stone. Ten feet long at the rectangular base with the stone itself centered between two permanently attached granite flower cups.

It was a nice stone at any price, Ellis thought as he pulled up a devil's trumpet vine trying to establish itself on his plot. So what if he wasn't dead yet, or even sick for that matter?

Where did it say in some damn etiquette book that you had to be dead to buy a tombstone, although he was fairly certain that somewhere there was one that said that very thing? Ellis breathed out heavily as he thought about how upset Clara had been when he had the stone set in the cemetery.

She never brought it up to him but he knew she thought about it often. And think about it, she did. To Clara it was a constant reminder for all the world to see that someday she would be going over to her eternal rest.

She always had an uneasy thought in the back of her mind about what death was going to be like and now she had a very constant physical reminder of the upcoming occasion every time that she went to church, the grocery store, the beauty parlor, anywhere which took her east of Highway 72 past the cemetery.

She always tried to avoid looking out the car window at it when she drove by but something always compelled her to at least take a quick glance in the hopes that it had somehow vanished overnight. God, where were thieves when you wanted them? But no matter how little she wanted that rock, the thieves wanted it less, and so there it stood on row ten of the cemetery beckoning to her year in and year out that sooner or later, it would finally win.

It almost made a mockery out of her with its hard, proud defiance as if to say, take your time, my dear friend. But some day. Someday, I will outlast you and you will end up here in my shade. Depression came easily to Clara anymore and she soon found a grocery store and a beauty parlor west on Highway 72.

Ellis finished tidying up his cemetery plot and slowly made his way back to the car. His left leg tended to drag ever so slightly as it had for the last seventeen years. The whole world believed that it was the result of a fall off of the back of the wood shed, well the whole world minus two.

If Big Al had caught him upstairs in Big Al's own house in Big Al's own bed with Big Al's own wife, he would have taken Big Al's own knife and cut off Ellis' own sex life forever. Therefore, the quick leap out the window into the brick-lined flowerbed.

He grimaced when he thought about the pain that shot through his body when he hip planted his still naked thigh onto the upturned end of one of those bricks.

However, he thought of Big Al more, so he managed to quietly finish pulling his pants up and stealing away into the darkness of the neighboring pine grove.

The doctor told him two days later that it was just a bad bruise, but Doctor Arbolt had been wrong on more diagnoses than he had been right. One only had to remember Bud's little finger for that proof!

That stone bruise eventually became a four-inch yellow and blue blotch bordered by a deep red ring of infection. Walking became out of the question and Ellis truly feared that the Lord was punishing him for sins of the flesh.

He seriously pondered on how the Lord dealt out his justice and what were the guidelines for what punishment. OK, six minutes of truly hard humping preceded by ten minutes of getting to know the woman. By punish-mental standards, did that equate to a stone bruise? He guessed not when the bruise turned black and blue. A bone chip, perhaps. Surely God, in his infinite mercy, would not take his leg for one outside piece of ass.

My God, two-thirds of all men would be walking around on crutches if that were the case. No, the bone chip should cover it, he reasoned. She wasn't even that great. Just laid there with her legs spread straight out with a grin on her face seeming to broadcast that her work relative to the situation was done while keeping her two work-hardened hands clamped on his flour white ass.

He didn't much like the feel of those calloused hands on his hips; they just didn't feel like the hands of a woman. He tried to push them off or at least around to his back where the skin wasn't as sensitive. But those meat hooks would still find their way back to where she had them before.

Ellis didn't let the hands distract him for long, though, for there were other bounties to enjoy that were truly worth his attention. Al's wife had a marvelous figure, not by a New York model's measure but by a real man's standard of beauty. Rather big-boned, yet shapely, soft, with large breasts and full thighs.

Ellis often wondered why anyone would want to hump a little thin woman with a figure like a teenaged boy which seemed to be all the rage these days. Al's wife's huge breasts were shimmying back and forth with each measured stroke. She seemed to like it that way, although she never opened her mouth or even flickered an eyelid to let him know that was the case.

Just laid there with that same complacent look. Still, it just heated him up that much more to look at those beautiful globes in motion and before long, he knew that he had better turn his attentions elsewhere, or this would become one of the shortest lays in history.

He turned and looked out the window to redirect his thoughts to something less disturbing while keeping that same steady rhythm.

Well, the dogwoods are certainly opening early this year; that could mean a good early garden. That would be good. Yes, that indeed would be very good. Look at that: Al painted his fence posts. Yellow.

Of all colors, yellow. That man must be color blind. Yes, that must be it. Color blindness. It's a terrible condition. Would have painted his John Deere tractor the same color if he hadn't stopped him. Oh my God, lady, please hold those jugs still! Better, yes much better.

Where was I? Oh yes, actually painted his two chimneys. Red. Painted his chimneys. Why would any fucking man in his fucking right mind paint his fucking chimneys? Oh God, honey, cover up those tits. Please! Chimneys, oh yea, chimneys, that's right, chimneys. Painted 'em red, god red, yea baby, fuck red. Posts, I meant fence posts, red fence posts. I wonder if he'll paint the grass next. The man was painting crazy! The man was plain crazy. The man was out in the driveway….

Lust is a strange phenomenon. It usually consumes the bodies involved and whitens out all other feelings, senses and emotions that one would normally experience. Except for sight. And what a sight it was as Ellis scrambled out of big Al's bed, gathering all the clothes he could find, except one sock and not so carefully made his way out of the bedroom window. Precious memories, how they linger, how they linger in my soul, Ellis hummed to himself.

Chapter Five

Old Resident: Bud Jackson and His Infamous Finger

Bud had a large farm, beef cattle, of course and planted as well as harvested his own feed. One sunny fall day, he was mowing hay along with sericea and lespedeza to prepare for baling when he felt the familiar drag on the mower attached at the back of the tractor via the hydraulic power take-off.

The turnbuckle connecting the tractor to the mower was wrapped up with a ball of weeds and hay, thus preventing it from spinning freely. There was only one thing to do: get out a knife and cut the vegetative matter loose. The gloves had to go because, as Bud liked to say, "You can't stick two fingers up your own ass with gloves on."

Not many found it funny but he did. So, Bud took off the gloves and cut and pulled at the plant ball until it slowly loosened its grip. There was, however, a problem that Bud didn't know about and was not at all prepared for.

A baby copperhead had gotten caught up with the hay and, as such was also wrapped up in that ball. Still very much alive and madder than hell. When he freed up the snake enough so it could move its head, it struck him hard on his little finger.

Both fangs got him. It wasn't a very big snake, so Bud decided to just go ahead and finish his job. Later that evening, when sitting down for supper, he mentioned he felt a bit dizzy.

It must have been that snake that bit me. His wife looked at him in disbelief. "What? What kind of snake?" "It was just a little copperhead." His wife practically went into hysterics. "You idiot! That's a poisonous snake!" "I know that but it was a small one." "It makes no difference. It's a poisonous snake!" Bud tried to change the subject but that wasn't happening. She ran out of the room returned five minutes later and announced that Doctor Arbolt was on his way.

When the good doctor got there, he assessed the situation, took Bud's blood pressure, looked into his eyes, then took out his scalpel and cut the finger from fang hole to fang hole. He then expertly sucked the blood from the incision. There was a flaw in this otherwise flawless procedure.

Six hours had passed since the bite. As such, the poison was probably closer to his big toe than to that little finger. Also, little fingers have a tendency to be little. That incision also cut the vein feeding blood to it as well as severed the nerves.

Within three weeks, the end of his finger started to turn black and had to be amputated. The snake venom went through his body and caused no further concern. There was some discussion about filing suit against old Doc Arbolt, which was quickly dismissed. He was the only doctor in that part of the county back then.

Besides, he could deliver babies, would slide prescriptions and loved children, so what the hell. No need to cut off your finger to spite your face.

Chapter Six
Builder Supervisor Allen Staton
Springfield Estates Groundbreaking

Allen Staton grabbed a pair of size 10 high-top rubber boots, slipped them on and headed for the front office door at Gleason Builders. Damn it, he thought to himself, why doesn't whoever used these things last clean the red mud off the bottoms of them.

He tried to walk gingerly across the floor but that didn't keep him from leaving a trail of hardened mud from the storage room all the way to the front door and then out into his truck.

He pulled out onto Morningside Dr, went through the gears and headed for the interstate. God, what a beautiful day! Of course, today, it could rain in sheets, and it would still qualify as a beautiful day. They were finally getting that subdivision going full bore at Springfield Estates.

He thought about all the times he had tried to buy land out there only to have the door slammed in his face. Springfield was the most logical place for development and every builder knew it. Every one of them had been out there only to get the same answer time and time again with each rejection getting more vocal and more threatening than the time before.

The new four-lane Highway 10 out of Asheville made the small town of Springfield quickly accessible. Also, Lake Morgan was just a twenty-minute drive away.

Yes sir, this was a can't miss opportunity with the right marketing campaign if I could just talk one of these local boys to relinquish more of their land. One step at a time, he said to himself. So far, the locals haven't burned down the site office trailer.

They had, however, pulled up every surveyor's stake, removed benchmark monuments as if the ground had swallowed them up, removed plastic marker flags and cut down temporary electric service entrance posts.

Ames Surveying had been out there so many times that they were calling the place their second home. The hostility from the locals bothered Allen a great deal and he knew that something had to be done to stop it as soon as possible.

He just didn't know what that was just yet. This thing could really get nasty when the building actually gets started. The thought of seeing #2 grade two by four studs being used to build Farmer Brown's hog pen would have been absurdly funny if it weren't for the fact that he would be the one supplying the lumber. Yes, something was going to have to be done.

In a short while, Allen was turning left into the freshly dozed entrance of what was soon to be known as Springfield Estates. Prices start in the eighties, he happily thought to himself as he stepped out of his truck. Almost immediately, he noticed one of the surveyors who was now always on the scene running up to him.

Oh shit, now what. "Mr. Staton, we've got a little problem out here that you need to know about." "That doesn't surprise me, Bill. What now?" "Well, it seems that one of your plow boyfriends left a little gift for the dozer operator last night."

"All right, damn it; don't leave me in suspense; what is it?" Alex snapped back and immediately realized he had been far too harsh in his reply. "Look, I'm sorry. There was no need to shoot the messenger. What's going on?" "It will be easier for you to see it than for me to describe it." The surveyor led the way and Allen obediently followed.

Howard Stewart, the private owner and operator was sitting on an overturned five-gallon bucket under the shade of a nearby chinquapin oak looking rather intently at his pride and joy, a Caterpillar C4.4 front dozing, rear bucket 130 horsepower earth mover which now included as one of its' options approximately 200 pounds of very fresh cow manure covering the running boards, the engine and especially the seat; where a one and a half feet carefully arranged pile of still dew laden cow shit was awaiting inspection by at least two dozen blow flies.

Howard spit his chewing tobacco juice onto the ground, slowly cut his eyes from his cherished dozer and watched as Allen and the surveyor approached. He finally spoke "Ain't that purty?" Allen took it all in for about three minutes and then walked back to his truck.

Upon arriving, he reached through the open window on the passenger side. He turned on the citizen's band radio, flicking the channel indicator to Emergency 9. "KA-6072 calling Springfield volunteer fire department, anybody home, come back?'

"Go ahead, KA-6072, we copy. What's the problem?" Allen continued, "We've got a small car fire out here off of 72 near the old Springfield place. Thought you'd like to know about it as it's getting out of hand. You will probably need a tanker and truck with hoses as it's starting to flare pretty good; you copy?"

"Roger KA-6072, we are on our way." "Good enough. I'll be out there at the highway to guide you in." The fire department responded, "We read you loud and clear and will look for you. What's your name, KA-6072?"

Allen thought for a minute and answered, "Bobby Smith." Within minutes, sure enough, the wail of an approaching fire engine could be heard in the distance. The Springfield Volunteer Fire Department covered the entire southern half of the county and truly did community service to all of the people in that area.

Naturally, they extinguished fires but it also was not uncommon to see them providing immediate first aid to auto accident victims, heart attacks and an occasional broken bone. They had even good-heartedly rescued a kitten or two from the tops of backyard trees.

Yes, these fine men did indeed provide many fine services for this fine community. However, up until now, they had never been called to fire hose down a shit-laden bulldozer. But after today, even that service could be added to their long list of good deeds.

A young volunteer cadet was the first to the station to get the truck and, as such was the first on the scene. He frowned at Allen when he arrived, as there was obviously no smoke and obviously no fire. He was unsure how to proceed and expressed his concerns to Allen.

He wanted to wait until the Chief got there to wash down the dozer. Allen smiled broadly and assured him that the Chief was fully aware of the situation and gave his OK to help out with this smelly problem.

The young cadet bought it and started connecting the hose to the tanker. In truth, it took less than five minutes for him to completely wash away the evidence. About fifteen minutes later, the Chief showed up and to say that he was upset at being called out on a false fire alarm would have been an understatement.

He threatened to bring charges against Allen. A suggestion that Allen promptly encouraged. It would be the perfect example to bring all of the problems that they were encountering to the public's eye.

"Yes sir, please press charges against me and better yet get the newspapers, radio and television news teams in on it as well; he bluffed. That would be even better.

Maybe that would prompt the county and state police to find out who's been committing all of these malicious acts of vandalism and help me to get some of these local boys behind bars.

Yes sir, Mister Fire Chief. Please press charges against me." The Chief, seeing this as a direct challenge, promised to do just that while his freshman fireman finished recurling the hose.

"Yes sir, that is exactly what I will do, press charges, yes sir! You, Mr. Staton, will be hearing from me again next time with the police." It was his turn to bluff.

After all, he knew exactly who was carrying out all of the mischief. After the Chief and his young fire fighter hastily backed up their vehicles, the Chief had the last word. "You will hear from me again." Allen never heard from him again.

Chapter Seven
Springfield Estates
Homecoming

When the dust settled, thirty-five houses were standing proudly in neat parallel rows down streets with almost comical names: Plantain Lane, Endive Drive, Parakeet Street. Already caravans of cars could be seen making their way to Springfield Estates to examine this country mecca up close and personal.

Station wagons, sports sedans and even taxi cabs started slowly streaming through the subdivision, which made the procession look like an unwanted parade to the quiet people of Springfield.

The four model homes were open to all interested, each represented by two broadly smiling sales agents, each outdoing the lies told by the other. Interest was indeed high. 12.9% fixed on a 30 year loan.

This did not deter the sales agents as they busied themselves pointing out the many wonderful features to anyone that wanted to know and even to a few that didn't.

Each home came fully equipped with available options such as quaint ceiling fans, decorative wallpaper, walk-in pantries just like in your grandmother's house, and even hardwood-like floors just like those seen in the old days when houses were built to last!

Both heads and phrases were being happily turned with relative ease and nobody seemed to mind. Prices were quoted with direct eye contact and sincerity that bordered on honesty and none seemed to be too high even when both parties knew that they were.

There was going to be a certain far-reaching status to living out here and all seemed to pick up on that vibe. All except the good people of Springfield who had lived there their whole lives. The prospective loved the trees and the large lots.

Those one-acre lots provided enough space for a garden even though very few of the newcomers knew if a tomato grew on a vine, bush, tree or shrub. Some even though tomatoes were some sort of fruit! All anyone could be absolutely sure of was that theirs came from the grocery store wrapped in cellophane, four to a package at twenty-nine cents a pound.

Even still, the freedom to grow those tomatoes if they wanted to hold a certain feeling to it excited everyone. The sales agents were well-trained and had an answer ready for any and all questions.

Can we have a dog? What about leash laws? Will there be curbside trash pick-up? NO? What do people around here do with their trash? The sales agents' brilliance was never more evident than it was when they convinced these prospective buyers that hauling their own trash would actually be for their own benefit.

"Folks, let me answer that question by first asking you a question. Tell me, why did Springfield Estates first interest you? Was it the yearning deep inside you to get back to a simpler lifestyle? Was it the desire to keep your children from growing up without smog in their lungs? Or was it for the peace of mind you will get by keeping your family away from big city crime?

Could it be all of the above as well as that feeling of adventure that burns in the hearts of all of us to do something a little different from the suburb status quo? He paused a little to let that message sink in and then continued.

"Folks, this is the answer to all of those desires. Sure, you'll sacrifice a few minor inconveniences such as trash pick-up and a McDonald's right at your back door but you will eliminate trash pick-up charges and picking up Big Mac containers in your driveway. For all you gain, don't you think the trade-off is worth it?

Five confirmed sales were made that very afternoon, with nine more under contract by the end of the month. Into the second week, interest in the development increased even further and base prices climbed to $90,000.

Normally, Gleason Realty would have waited until the entire development was sold out before opening phase two. An exception was made in this case. For one, interest in the development was indeed very high and "number two", no one knew how the locals would react once the influx began.

It proved to be a good decision. Springfield Estates provided handsome profits for the builder, the builder's subcontractors, the tax assessors, the sales agents and the lenders.

Everyone was happy except for the local folks who began to look at each car going into that cursed subdivision as a troop carrier coming to lay siege on their happy town.

One thing was for sure: things would never be the same for Springfield's old or new residents.

Chapter Eight
Springfield Estates
If Only There Was A McDonald's Nearby

Within a period of twelve months, every home in Springfield Estates was fully occupied. Each family was busy adding distinctive touches to their piece of heaven to make it feel more like home.

A wind chime hanging on a six sectioned bird house sitting above a three-tiered bird bath with a working fountain seemed to be the favorite with the group. The birds however would never go near the thing because it scared the hell out of them.

Barbeque grills started sending out their smoke signals every Saturday afternoon while television satellite dishes sprouted up like wild dandelions in each and every backyard.

The women in the development would dig around their flowers and shrubs every evening in the spring in their white shorts with matching pastel-colored knit shirts.

The menfolk would busy themselves by mowing the lawn with their newly purchased sixteen horsepower riding lawnmowers, which absolutely astounded all the local men in the area.

"Damn, he's got more horses under the hood of that lawn mower to cut his joke of a yard than I use to cultivate my ten acres of soybeans, "John commented to Arthur as they drove through Springfield Estates one Saturday afternoon. "And just look at that grass. That's pathetic. Can you believe that just last year; Evan had this entire cleared portion planted in sericea and lespedeza? He is rolling over in his grave right now, I tell you."

There was a genuine aura of sadness shared between them. "And look at their dogs. What in the hell do you make that thing out to be?" he said while pointing at a long-haired Pekinese gingerly making its way across a hot concrete drive. "I'm sure that someone with mischief on their mind would kick in that front door, take a look at that yipping dog and then pass out cold from laughing too hard. Maybe that's the plan."

John laughed but also felt his stomach knot. "Arthur, do you think there is one man in this whole damn outfit that has done an honest day's work in his entire life, just one?" Arthur had already had that thought and concluded that not one had.

"No, I can guarantee that if you looked at any one of 'ems hands they would be as soft as a young woman's. And can you imagine living packed together like sardines in a can, all jammed up beside each other like this? Good God, I would go out of my mind." John agreed, and they rode along in silence.

"John, you and I now, we could never live like this, no way but they can and don't seem to mind it. So I can't figure out why all of these people came all this way to live out here, all cramped up when they could have stayed in town and been just as cramped up there. It just doesn't make sense to me." He let out a long sigh. "I don't know, man. I'm sure each has their own story to tell."

Chapter Nine

Soon To Be New Resident
Jack Owens and His Daughter Kelly

Good God, what could possibly be the holdup now? If I don't accelerate and cool this engine down some, that radiator is going to do its' number again and I'll be walking.

He could envision the headlines: a man in a three-piece suit has a stroke walking along Interstate 87. His family doctor had told him just hours before that his blood pressure had not reached seriously elevated levels yet. However, if he didn't start relaxing more, he could very well be heading for a potentially dangerous condition.

Loosely translated, 'don't sweat the small stuff and realize that everything is small stuff'. Jack forced himself to stop worrying about the traffic and exhaled slowly and deeply, realizing that getting all worked up wasn't going to make that car ahead of him move any faster than it was now.

It seemed that lately, everything upset him and no matter how hard he tried, he couldn't find that inner satisfaction with anything anymore. And lately, little sayings and remembered verses from his younger days would unexplainably pop into his mind and stay there for hours to be mentally repeated over and over.

'What used to be a blazer is now ivy league'. Hell, he didn't even know what that meant but he remembered he heard it on the old Jimmy Dean variety show when he was just a kid.

For some reason, when whoever had belted out that line he locked it in his memory to bring out at times when he needed to keep his mind occupied. Up until he was twenty-five, he had spent all of that idle time daydreaming about sex with any woman he was even remotely interested in.

His mind was almost always directly dialed to a hard-on. And now? 'What used to be a blazer is now ivy league'. He could understand replacing idle mind time with something more spiritually uplifting than sex as he grew older, but to revert to mindless idle chatter?

It did upset him and he actually chastised himself when he caught himself repeating gibberish. Jack signaled his intentions and turned into the azalea-lined entrance of Parkwood Plaza Apartments, the family refuge from the world for the past six years.

Good, Patty's already home, he thought to himself as he pulled into the parking space beside her Firebird. Already home. Home right? Home is where the heart is. The heart, a family of cockroaches, sporadic hot water, and two young married couples just a two by four stud and two pieces of sheetrock away. Home.

Sometimes, Jack felt like just turning around as soon as he arrived, but then where would he go? Back to the bank? God forbid. Sometimes, Jack wished that some street-hardened thugs would blow the safe and accidentally do in the building as well.

God, how he hated that place. He had little to no tolerance for that stupid saying, 'You have the right job when your vocation is your vacation' when he knew it should go like this: 'The place where you toil for wealth is actually ruining your health'.

Working at the bank was monotonous. The co-workers were all climbers and the overall aura was one of forced friendliness, which tended to turn Jack's insides into acid. What bothered him more was that he slowly developed that same phony attitude.

Sometimes when a particularly pompous depositor was sharing his high and mighty financial predictions, Jack would silently be screaming every nasty obscenity he could think of back at him.

Of course, on the surface, he was all professionalism and diplomacy. Everybody thought of Mr. Owens as a nice guy, except Jack. The great compromiser, the man with no inner conviction, the bender with the winder, the 'Me and my gal went blackberry pickin'. Sometimes, he just wanted to cry, but he had forgotten how on his 25th birthday and hadn't been able to turn out a tear ever since.

Jack put the key in the lock and then remembering that Patty was home, just grabbed the door knob, turned it and pushed inward. He nearly broke his wrist when nothing gave. "Damn it, Patty!" he shouted as he vigorously shook his left wrist.

Once inside, he started for the kitchen to give her hell when reason finally took over and convinced himself that she was only doing the sensible thing by keeping the doors locked. He breathed in and out and chastised himself for acting so childishly. "Hi, hon." Patty sang out as she came through with a basket of dirty clothes.

"You aren't getting off that easily'' Jack grabbed her around the waist and kissed her while she maneuvered the basket out of the way to make room for him. "How has your day been?" "Oh, you know. Same old, same old, yours?"

"About the same where's Kelly?" "Taking a nap." Patty pulled away slightly and Jack let her go. It was the same scenario that had been played out every afternoon for some time.

Words that must be said. Jack subconsciously knew that he and Patty didn't share their thoughts anymore. But he just rationalized that no married couple was into the game for as long as they had been. And maybe it was good that they didn't. Keeping a few secrets from each other was probably a good thing.

Jack picked up the afternoon paper from the foyer table and headed for the Barcalounger Kelly had given him for Father's Day a few years ago. A handmade card titled 'I Lave You, Dady' had been taped to the armrest. Jack kept that card among his valuable papers locked in their safety deposit box that the bank had given him as a perk when he was promoted to Credit Manager.

Most people get bonuses when they are promoted; I get a friggin lock box. How about giving me something to put in that lock box he said to himself. Oh well, what the hell. Kelly entering the room brought him back to reality.

"Hello, Kelly-girl. Do you have a kiss for Daddy?" She rolled her sleepy eyes up to him and came to him with arms open wide. He kissed her cheek and held her close, his tensions melting away with each passing second. She had that internal peace about her, much like her mother did.

"Have you been a good girl today?" "Um-hum," she replied while grabbing his hand with both of hers and swinging backward on her heels. She held her head back and let her long brunette hair hang free down her back.

God, she is going to be a heart breaker one of these days, just like her mother. Her natural grace and peaceful nature set her head and shoulders apart from everybody else her own age, again just like her mother. It suddenly dawned on him that she had very few of his outward qualities at all.

Damn, I guess she's mine. No, he knew that she was. Back when Kelly was conceived there were no two people on this earth that loved each other as much as he and Patty had.

For five solid years, he never had one bad day, regardless of the events that occurred. He had Patty, and she loved him with all of her heart; that was all that mattered.

They could get caught in the most trying circumstances and it would only give them another event they could tell others they shared together. They never fought; they never even argued. Nothing in the world was worth upsetting her.

She had a girlish laugh back then that she despised that would break out at spontaneous times of happiness that would literally make him dizzy with love. He loved the laugh all the more if it was brought about by something he did or said because there could be no denying her feelings at the time; so genuine was the joy that it revealed in her.

He hadn't heard that laugh in a long time and wondered if he ever would again. He knew that Patty still loved him though lately she slipped into moods that he didn't understand and at the same time knew he wasn't welcome in.

On those intervals, she would smile at him distantly and he knew that any amount of prodding on his part would reveal anything more than she was willing to show on the surface. She wouldn't get mad; she just wouldn't give up anything.

So he would finally concede and leave her with her thoughts. It was always lonely in the house during these times she was away, even more so when she would let Kelly into her mind-world. Oh well, such is the price one has to pay when one makes a lifetime commitment. Jack would learn to tell that lie to himself with greater frequency with each passing year.

Jack returned to his newspaper. He went from page to page, aimlessly skimming stories for something he might find mildly interesting. A quarter-page ad grabbed his attention.

Springfield Estates Something Different For People Who Demand More

The ad went into great detail describing shaded lanes, large developed lots, paved streets with curb and guttering, beautiful contemporary styled homes and country living with few restrictions, all carefully developed, designed and built by award-winning Gleason Builders & Realty.

Gleason was indeed one of the few builders in the Asheville market area with a solid reputation for building quality homes. You paid for that as their homes carried a premium price.

Jack not so carefully tore out the ad and folded it to fit in his shirt pocket. He then set the paper aside and pulled down the lever to adjust the chair horizontally. He then closed his eyes and tried to imagine himself as a homeowner. God, it would be nice to have a large screened porch and maybe a workshop full of tools that he didn't know how to use, as well as a garage.

But most of all, he wanted privacy, which always seemed to be a commodity reserved for the rich. Apartment living provides you with little to no privacy inside or out. If a favorite song came on the radio, especially one that sounded better at a higher volume, the temptation to crank it up would soon be overruled by the dull thud of a broom handle against the wall.

And just once, he would like to hear Patty really let herself go when they were in bed together. Even when she was really heated up, she would keep herself bottled up for the benefit of the neighbors. Just once, he would love to see her completely let go and scream like a banshee if she felt so inclined.

Jack carefully rubbed both of his eyes with the palms of his hands and then slowly opened his eyes. He watched Kelly as she walked over to the television set. Using the remote control, she turned it on and started going from channel to channel.

The reception had been so bad in the apartment complex that they had to subscribe to cable whether they wanted to or not. All at the additional living expense of thirteen dollars per month. Jack had hated the apartment living from the very beginning.

However, on their young upwardly mobile salaries, it was an apartment or living with one of their parents, especially after Kelly was born. Their entire married life had been in flats, duplexes, apartments or townhomes. Kelly had never known anything else.

She didn't know the joys of having a dog, even a swing set in the back yard.

Jack kept telling Patty that someday when he had a more secure job, when they were financially independent, when the interest rates came down, when Kelly turned twenty-eight or when the banks started giving houses away then maybe they could afford a place of their own.

There were just so many variables, so many unknowns, so many chances that one had to live with when your name was attached to a thirty-year mortgage.

Thirty years! Jack always felt uneasy when he thought about all of the disasters that could befall a homeowner when layoffs occurred when sickness cleaned out a savings account when the well pump blew and the roof had to be replaced at the same time.

I'm only looking for guarantees, Jack reasoned with himself, and I of all people should know that life never comes with one.

Chapter Ten

Jack's Wife Patty

What Channel Are You Watching?

Patty carefully bit on the inside of her lip as she finished ironing the collar of Jack's favorite white shirt with the mallard duck on the breast pocket. 50-50 poly/cotton blend, machine wash, tumble dry. She slipped the ironed shirt over a wooden hanger and hung it on the edge of the board.

She quickly glanced up at the art deco clock that they had bought on sale at Richway and realized that she had twenty minutes until American Bandstand came on. Thirty-two, and she still watched Bandstand.

Must be a glutton for punishment, she thought to herself as she got started on the next shirt. These girls today start younger and show more than we ever did at their age.

Am I wrong, or do these young girls look for guys to give it up to? That was the perception she had and she was pretty sure that she was right.

Many nights here recently, she had carefully examined herself in front of the full-length mirror and realized that, indeed, she was getting older.

Small cellulite marks snaked their way across the lower part of her once finely toned ass and the fleshy portion of her inner thighs were decidedly more fleshy than she had remembered. Still, all in all not too bad. The hourglass was still there, it's just that some of the sand had shifted; she smiled to herself at the thought.

She carefully cupped her breasts in both hands and lifted them upward slightly to the angle that she had seen them not so long ago. Damn it, she thought, why do women get old and ugly while men get old and distinguished.

Gone to seed was the term she overheard a group of men say among themselves when describing another woman in the office. Gone to seed. How many years did she have left before they used that term to fit her description?

Her stomach twisted in repulsion at the thought and she became bitterly vehement in her thoughts to those and all men on the planet. She felt the need to cry; her eyes slowly welled up in tears that started tracing lines down her cheeks.

All of a sudden, her naked body appeared distorted and ugly to her and she hurried to throw a robe around her shoulders. She wanted comfort and security that only a kind, caring man with strong arms could provide. Her thoughts never once went to Jack.

Patty sat down on the king-size bed in her robe and picked up the ad for Springfield Estates that she had cut out of last week's

Sunday paper. There was a new subdivision being built not too far away that sounded heavenly to her.

It was fun to cut it out and daydream about it, even though she knew it would eventually go straight into the trash can. Jack was already emotionally wound up tighter than a rubber band; adding this to his plate would serve no purpose. She sighed and picked up the latest issue of Cosmopolitan.

If I'm going to daydream may as well daydream big. She nonchalantly thumbed through the pages until she caught a glimpse of a Maiden form advertisement. 'I dreamed I went to Bali in my Maiden form bra'.

The ad made no sense to her whatsoever. Not one Maiden form ad that she had ever seen did. But the picture of a middle aged woman in a pair of floral panties and a small French cut bra in a jungle did stir something in her.

Not that she had a thing about running around naked in a jungle. The woods nearby would do just fine. Free and naked and wild and untamed and hungry to be taken by a very virile, handsome man who didn't threaten. She threw the magazine back into the rack beside the bed as she eased her hips down into the sheets.

Patty met Jack at Carolina back in the turbulent 60's when both were hell bent on integration, equal rights and freedom to all people, peace in the world and a purging of corruption in government.

They frequented sit-ins, had been arrested together, went to rock concerts and even formed a rock band for a short period of time. She had long, straight hair that Jack told her reminded him of a brunette Joan Baez.

He played the guitar, played it well, and sang with so much conviction that Patty knew that she would love him forever or at least for seven years as it turned out, which was just about right according to her Grandpa's Timetable.

She sometimes wished that she didn't know anything about that crazy timetable now that she knew for sure that it wasn't just a nerve impulse misfire in an old man's head. Life had proven it to be accurate too many times.

She remembered when she was a mischievous little girl who couldn't stand still for more than two minutes at a time. Grandpa Jenkins was sitting in the high-back oak rocker in the backyard, just rocking and smiling as he watched her playing alone in the shade of the large elms that made up the back yard of the old home place.

Never had he seen a child that could be so content all by herself with only her mind as her toys. Truly a gifted child. A peaceful warmth filled his chest with love as he watched her bend down to pick a long-stemmed plantain and come running toward him to make him the target of it.

He feigned as she "pointed" the tip of it at him and pulled the now folded stem. The flower hit him in the arm, which delighted the child and made her laugh aloud as he closed his eyes and dropped his head down onto his chest.

She bent over and kissed him on the cheek, which instantly brought him back to life as it had every single time the scene had been enacted. "Patty-Cake, come sit with your old grandpap for a while."

Patty awkwardly lowered herself to the ground beside him without a word. "Little girl, you are growing like one more weed. Did you not know that? Why, it seems like just yesterday that I was rocking you in this chair and now look at you.

All grown up. Are you married yet?" he asked and winked at her at the same time. Patty just giggled and pretended to hit him. "No, Patty, I know you aren't married yet but you will be before you know it."

But some changes have to take place before you do. And those changes are right around the corner. Baby girl, you are fixing to shed your old skin and change into something more wonderful than you are now, if that's possible.

"Grandpa, you aren't making any sense at all. I ain't going to shed my skin like an old lizard." Her grandfather roared with laughter in approval as if that was just how he knew that she would reply.

His eyes still twinkling, he continued. "My dear, you have already changed once and you are due for another very soon. Every seven years in your life, you will have a complete mental, physical and emotional channel change, just like on a TV set. Flick the knob once you have a western, again a comedy, again a fuzzy screen. Same picture tube but different images. You, my dear, are just like that TV set. And once every seven years, life will change the channel. At birth, life was blown into your lungs, and life turned on the set. You were totally dependent on your parents and though you had eyes and could see, you were blind to everything. Total dependence. Then, at seven, life turned the knob once. While still very dependent, you questioned everything, driving your parents crazy with all of your questions. Just like you just questioned my seemingly foolish statement just a few minutes ago. And, very soon, life will turn the channel again. And life will again do wonderful things to you. I won't tell you about that change now, for everyone would call me a dirty old man, but even still, remember my words, my priceless little buttercup."

He paused briefly to determine if his words were getting through to this brassy little angel. When she remained quiet, he knew that they had. His eyes laughed, and he continued on a more serious note. "Patty, there is one thing that you must remember about these changes. You must never try to readjust the knob back to a past channel. No matter how wonderful that time was, you must remember that you can never go backward. To try would only bring unhappiness and heartache and rob you of the joys you could be experiencing in this new time in your life."

And so it had been.

As Patty lay on the bed, she couldn't help but smile as she thought of the old man's words. She thought of the change at 14. OK, so he missed it by a year; he was still pretty close. At 21. What at 21? She had Kelly at 21. Damn.

Yet still, she was rebellious and searching. At 28, giving up the search and becoming happy with raising their daughter. Going to work in the real world and developing a career, not a job, a career. Getting a job as a secretary at an ad agency in Asheville. Moving shortly from a secretary to a photographer's aide due to her creative tendencies. From there to a layout artist and color print coordinator.

Up to now, an advertising manager. She was the best they had ever had and they knew it. Yep, it was a great position that she loved, she thought to herself. Still, something was puzzling her and for the life of her, she couldn't define it.

She had a beautiful 'almost too good to be true' daughter, a great career and a husband who loved her. Jack the guitarist, the long-haired guitarist from two changes ago. And then it dawned on her what was bothering her.

Even though now Jack was a credit manager at a local bank, in her mind he was still and would always be the guitar playing 'love of her life' from a time when she was just a rebellious young girl.

And try as she might, she could not convert the image of Jack from guitarist boyfriend to credit manager husband. She also couldn't help but wonder if he looked at her in the same way, in the same time frame. She slowly closed her eyes and felt her chest get heavy. "Grandpa", she said aloud, "please change the channel".

Chapter Eleven
Ode to All the Harrys' in the World

Back at the office, it was apparent to everyone that Harry was a very misunderstood soul. Some wanted to intervene to help the dear man but instinctively knew that there was a real chance that his entire burden could end up completely falling on their own shoulders.

As such, no one was willing to take that first step. In truth, Harry was very much an inwardly focused person. Unfortunately for him, he didn't like what he saw. So to compensate, he would search out the bad in others and then wonder why people avoided him.

He did have a sense of humor, but it was so dry that it almost bordered on not being funny. But, because so few people really knew him, everyone winced at his attempts at humor as nothing more than sarcasm.

Harry would sometimes valiantly attempt his hand at spontaneous wit only to be stonewalled more often than not by blank, inquisitive faces that would cut him to the quick and leave him flush with frustration.

Only once in as far back as he could remember had anyone ever laughed at one of his jokes. A new designer at the office had once openly laughed at one of his clever quips only to be quickly silenced by everyone else in the room by their unbelieving stares at her.

Without a word spoken, she had clearly learned that if she was going to "fit in" she would never laugh at a single word that Harry ever spoke going forward. She learned quickly and well because from that time on, she avoided him as if he was carrying any number of highly transmittable social diseases.

So, at times, when he truly felt the need for an open release of his emotions, he would sit right down and write himself a letter, a sonnet or a poem. People seemed to accept this as accepted introverted behavior because it required absolutely no input from them on any level.

It was funny to Harry that anyone who painted, composed or attempted any form of creative expression that required no direct contact with anyone was automatically considered an introvert. Harry had never met a soul that admitted to being an introvert; that was always a title placed upon someone delivered by others, often with an air of disdain.

Any introvert alive was just a person frustrated by the inability to make friends, which, compounded by popular opinion of all the rest of the world who were all friends, soon left one with absolutely no one to talk to except other introverts who tended not to talk much.

Harry would have marveled at the simple truth of that statement if it weren't for the fact that they truly defined his life.

He knew he had to be careful who he talked to but more importantly who he listened to, especially if one was an introvert. Harmful words heard had defined his life and had seeped into every synapse in his brain.

They were like dear old friends that never wanted to leave him. On occasion, he would mentally rise up against them; however, they instinctively knew when to back off, melt away and hide in deep recesses in his mind.

He had recently purchased a self-help book that seemed to make sense to Harry. It outlined how some of us reincarnated from past lives. Actions, both good and bad from that past life carried into the current one. It really made him think about his life.

Damn, I must have been a hell of a guy the last go around or maybe the time before! He thought to himself, 'My God Harry, did you rape a Popes' mama, did you stone Stephen, help Doctor Mendela, did you shoot Archduke Ferdinand? Did you pick a fight with Martin Luther? Were you Cain back in the beginning of all of this? Did you dance around the golden calf? Or was it all of the above?

What if all truly bad things were done by just a select few predestined to carry out dirty deeds with each new turn in life? Was

I a slave trader on the Ivory Coast making my fortune on the blood of innocent people? Was I Pilate, Judas, or Nero? The antichrist, the serpent in the apple tree?' It would explain things like why he had to work twice as hard to get at best half the credit.

Just the past week, he had finished a poem that he had been working on for several weeks and he actually found some degree of comfort in it. He thought it was clever and wanted to share it with his colleagues at work but immediately realized what a bad idea that was.

He titled it 'Exercise Your Futility.'

Why even try? It's all a lie, a game inside your mind

It's an endless fight for the not-so-bright 'cause the blind do lead the blind

Call it a rat race. You give me last place. I'll let you direct the show.

You'll climb the ladder to whom will it matter when you're lying six feet below.

But love is the answer, sang the song and dancer, only who recalls the question.

'Cause people change which can rearrange that love into a new direction.

So keep your eyes where the real truth lies on the things life cannot bend.

Give no guarantees, live life as you please, let the means justify your end.

The more he concentrated on the words of that poem, the darker his thinking became. He did have a plan B in life that he revealed to no one. It was in a box in the back of his bedroom closet.

A blued steel Smith and Wesson Model 10 Snub Nosed .38 Special with a fifty-round box of hollow point bullets. He had thought about suicide on a few particularly bad occasions but always remembered his father's words before he had died. 'Life is short and precious. It is given to you as a gift, and you have no right to throw it away'.

Having said that, his dad suffered greatly towards the end of his life and modified his advice somewhat. 'You still can't take your own life but you could bargain with God by letting him know that if He wanted to take you home early, you would be OK with it'.

Sometimes, Harry felt that was all he had going for him. The every night prayer 'that if God wanted to take him home early, he would be OK with it'.

Please God. Tonight, maybe tomorrow night. I would be OK with it. But it seemed to him that God after all was a very busy fellow and had little time available to listen to his pleas.

Chapter Twelve
Harry's Moving Day

Harry did have one thing working in his favor. His father had set up a $50,000 whole life insurance policy on himself the year that Harry was born. When his father died, he as beneficiary received the proceeds which was a great deal of money at that time.

He invested somewhat conservatively but still had accrued a net worth of over $85,000. The lease on his apartment was about up and the apartment manager had already warned him that there would be a fifteen percent increase for the coming year.

He had seen the newspaper ad about Springfield Estates and it piqued his curiosity. He had entertained the idea of just picking up and starting over as if hitting an imaginary reset button would change his life.

He sat down with the branch manager at his bank who explained to him that he could have a very low monthly payment, much lower than his current apartment rent by simply making a down payment for the house from his current savings account.

His banker even joined him when he went out to the Springfield Estates sales office. The whole process went remarkably smoothly. The salesman doted on Harry like they were best friends.

Harry liked it! He even opened a bottle of champagne and all at the table had a throwaway plastic wine glass full once the details were ironed out.

As an added bonus the salesman even agreed to pay for all moving expenses just because he liked him. Yes, the starting over idea was working pretty good so far, Harry thought to himself.

Allen Staton, the builder met with Harry at his new house after all had been completed and the final punch list had been satisfied. He then went over everything and showed him how everything worked.

Harry genuinely couldn't believe how nice everyone and everything was. There was a new home warranty included so he only had to contact Allen if there were any issues at all.

After every question and concern had been addressed, he gave the house keys to Harry, shook his hand and left. Harry stood there alone wondering what to do next.

What little furniture he owned had already been dropped off that morning along with six large cardboard boxes marked KITCHEN, Baths, MASTER BEDROOM, CLEANING SUPPLIES, And BOOKS 1 AND 2. He had carried anything electronic with him in the back seat of his car.

Earlier in the day, he had dropped off the keys to his apartment at the complex office. He explained his reason for leaving and assured them it had nothing to do with the apartment itself.

He told them that he had enjoyed his five years living there and would leave with fond memories. He smiled broadly for added emphasis. The office manager gave him a puzzled look and asked him who he was.

Finally, she spoke, "OK, yea sure. Where do you want the security deposit mailed to?" Harry smiled and thought to himself that this was indeed a fitting sendoff. Mail it to Harry Campo, 402 Plantain Lane, Springfield, NC 26199.

Chapter Thirteen

The Accident

Miracles Come In Many Shapes and Sizes

The constant buzzing of the alarm clock in his left ear finally woke Harry from his deep sleep. He groped around for the source of the noise and soon located the clock.

With all four forefingers, he managed to find the alarm stem and pushed inward until the noise stopped. Damned alarm clock, he thought to himself as he shook the cobwebs out of his head and managed to pull himself up to a setting position in the bed. He glanced over to the clock to see the time and then changed his mind.

He knew that it was 7:02; he had gotten up at 7:02 for the last seven years. Even on weekends. Harry pulled back the comforter and stood up, stretched a few times deeply scratched his backside and then headed to the bathroom.

He stopped at the sink for a few seconds to throw some water in his face then made his way to the toilet to relieve himself. Without thinking about it, he turned on the shower, adjusted the water temperature with his fingers and then headed back to the sink to shave and brush his teeth.

It took Harry exactly thirty-one minutes to get from waking up to completely dressed, so regimented was his morning ritual of getting ready for work. The sequence of events were so orchestrated that he knew exactly what had to be done without really giving much thought at all.

Any additional requirements to this procedure would more often than not be forgotten. There were days that he had left his watch at home because he had failed to put it in its designated place the night before.

However, this morning was going to be different from most. In the comfort of his new home, he finally had read that self-help book from cover to cover. It outlined how to break out of damaging negative habits and he vowed to give it a try.

At some point during his shower, it dawned on him that this was the day he would be putting those steps into practice. At first, he balked at the idea after weighing out the hopelessness of the situation but then decided, why not. What do I have to lose? And it might just work at that. I will not let a soul get to me today. I won't care what they say. Give me your worst world. I can take it.

After a while, Harry actually started to believe what he was thinking and a fire of determination started kindling in his chest. You know, I do feel good this morning, he thought to himself as he finished toweling himself off. I really do!

Damned good as a matter of fact. You know, my mind really is my worst enemy, he concluded. If I think I'm nothing, then the world will think I am nothing. So it stands to reason, he said to himself as he sat down, that if I think I'm worthy then the world will as well.

"And if I think that I'm daam-ed good then the world better look out", he sang aloud while straightening his tie and throwing his head back in front of the mirror.

He looked at himself for a few minutes and then grinned at his image in the mirror, reflecting a reverse image of himself. "You know Harry; you really aren't such a bad looking fellow. Work out with some weights for a while and the women may well go wild."

He tried to picture himself as a macho man and then laughed. Who knows? "Harry, my friend, let's go slay some dragons. Your kingdom awaits you." He then grabbed his briefcase and headed out the door, turning off the front porch light on his way out. God, it's a beautiful day he thought to himself and couldn't help but smile at the thought.

When was the last time I thought it was a beautiful day, he wondered. Hell, I don't have beautiful days. I mean the old Harry didn't have beautiful days; this Harry will have at least three beautiful days a week.

He was almost giddy by the time he had backed his Datsun out of the driveway. As he made his way down Plantain Lane, he couldn't help but notice the man who lived next door walking out to his newspaper box at the end of his driveway.

Quickly, his joy turned sour as the familiar knot of distrust gripped his heart and he felt his breathing starting to get shallow. He could only imagine how much the man didn't like him.

He probably enjoyed not having a house right next door and I ruined that for him. Harry thought about just looking straight ahead without even looking his way as he approached the street, even though he knew deep down that he should at least nod at him as he went by.

He felt his hands grip the wheel tightly as his heart started pounding in his chest. OK, nod. I'll nod his way and then quickly look back to the road without knowing whether he acknowledged the nod by returning the nod with a nod. That was the way he would have handled that type of situation before. And then it dawned on him that this was supposed to be a new Harry. The old Harry nodded.

This new Harry will stop the car, roll down the window and chat with his neighbor for a few minutes. He breathed deeply and allowed determination to overtake the fears in his mind. That determination was shot to hell by the time that he reached the Harriston's mailbox.

He quickly nodded at Walter as he went by and then quickly looked back to the road without knowing whether Walter acknowledged the nod with a nod.

Big change, new Harry, new start. You stupid fool, Harry thought to himself as he stopped the car at the stop sign on two-lane Highway 72.

Mister dragon slayer, you don't even have the guts to speak to your own neighbor. He felt all of the new walls of strength that he had constructed deconstruct with one not so mighty blow.

He wanted to just turn the car around and go back home, taking another day of sick leave but was afraid that Walter may still be at his paper box. He felt tears burn his eyes as he pulled out onto the highway, pushing down on the accelerator with more pressure than necessary which caused his right rear tire to squeal.

Dammit, now the neighbors will think you're some sort of juvenile. Can't you do anything right, no wonder everyone hates you, you big loser. He wanted to hide, to just somehow disappear. He would never be able to handle life. There was no denying it, he said to himself even though there was no other soul in the car.

Harry the dragon slayer. He couldn't resist savagely attacking his own ego for even entertaining the thought. Harry finally focused his thoughts back on his driving long enough to realize that the Ford pickup ahead of him was creeping down the road at about fifteen miles per hour.

He started braking as he glanced at his speedometer. Forty-five miles per hour. He braked even harder and saw the blur of an Oldsmobile behind him accelerate to pass both him and the pickup. As soon as the Oldsmobile cleared him, Harry followed it after it cleared his car. Suddenly the Olds sped up.

The Ford truck locked his brakes after clearing…what the hell is that? And Harry had nowhere to go. His eyes opened wide as both feet slammed down hard on the brake pedal. He steered as hard as he could into the shoulder of the highway, at the same time bracing for the inevitable collision.

Each time a breeze kicked up, long stalks of Johnson grass brushed against Harry's cheek through his open driver-side window slowly bringing Harry back into the real world 'Springfield standard time'.

He came to half startled, coming out from a dreamy, surreal world into a real-world far more absurd than any his mind could have ever conjured up. Harry slowly raised his head from the steering wheel, opened his eyes and tried to force himself to concentrate.

He knew he wasn't waking from a night of sleep, even though he felt no pain, no discomfort at all actually. When his eyes finally focused, he was unsure of where he was or what had happened. Looking out to his left brought him into a world of tall grass, small ladybugs, blue sour-smelling buds of roadside chicory and an empty Budweiser can.

To his right, the world was altogether different with many abstract faces staring down at him; not a single smile in the group. Looking straight ahead brought him immediately out of the haze and made him painfully aware of his surroundings.

As he let it all sink in, his breathing became shallow and he turned pale. His whole troubled life all of a sudden seemed meaningless due to this one moment. Every petty difference, sullen misunderstanding and exaggerated problem that had chased him throughout his life fled from his mind like cowards in this one single incident.

Harry had struck a tractor as best as he could tell from behind with his Datsun. The driver of the tractor was apparently laying off at the edge of the street under a huddled mass of people and Harry instinctively knew he was dead.

I've killed a man; the thought made its' way right into the center of his mind and then carried the news down to his heart. Oh my dear God, I've killed a man.

The ominous thought of such a thing being a reality helped him find the strength to scramble out the side window of the car. The car had plowed into a ditch after hitting the tractor, cutting a gash about ten feet long into the embankment.

I'm lucky I'm not dead, Harry thought to himself after surveying the damage to his car, which was quite extensive. Considering his situation, he thought I would be better off dead.

This was major trouble and he knew it. Any other time he would have relished the moment to be mentally melodramatic but this time the situation was serious.

He could waste no time on what he now realized had been a lifetime of childish emotion-fed mind games. It dawned on Harry the enormity of this revelation in his life at such a time that this should have been expanded and carefully analyzed for the importance of the message that it carried, but there was no time.

He had to make his way over to the mass of people which surrounded something that Harry could only surmise was the body of the man whose soul Harry had whisked away just minutes before.

"What in the damn hell did you have your mind on, boy?" A firm hand grabbed his shoulder from behind, which almost brought Harry to his knees; not due so much due to fright but surprise. Harry whirled around in startled trepidation, wondering what new circumstances were about to bombard his already overtaxed senses.

The angry face he now faced looked vaguely familiar, even though he had no idea where he had seen this person before. The thought that he may know him seemed doubtful to him.

How could he? He stared at the face intently hoping for a clue as to how he knew this burly stranger who still had a lock on his shoulder.

"I asked you a damn question, boy? Were you trying to kill me back there?" Back there? Harry eyed the man carefully from head to toe. Tall, about sixty, broad in the shoulder, earthy, healthy, flannel shirt, work jacket, worn jeans with a bloodied stain from knee to hip on his right leg.

"Was that you on the tractor that I hit? Oh, thank God!" Harry exhaled loud and long and made no attempt to hide his relief. "What the hell do you mean thank God, you little bastard? You could have killed me back there or is that what you are trying to do?" His voice bellowed. "I ought to beat the hell out of you right now.

That's what I ought to do, just beat the hell out of you right now. Cause if you were, take a good look at this leg because this is how your whole body is going to look when I'm finished with you."

The man driving the tractor was not dead, only bruised. He was not under that huddle of people; he was right there standing in front of him, threatening to change the natural contours of his face.

Harry's brain understood and rejoiced at the thought. No one was killed, and minor bruises as best he could tell.

Drop back and punt, end of down, but the quarter's not even over. Melodrama slowly crept back into its' rightful place and rationalization crumbled without resistance.

Harry was startled at the intensity of the injured man's eyes, burning through him like a torch. Their message was familiar to him: hate, hate unfitting the circumstance as far as Harry could see. However, hate he knew and also knew how to react to it. His reaction was unconditional and spontaneous.

Even the now very much alive tractor driver was taken aback by Harry's reaction. Harry's eyes glazed now that the danger appeared over. His fear of the big man was genuine; his glazed doleful eyes were bona fide indicators of that.

Instinctively he squeezed the last hint of emotion out of the situation. His voice broke, his heart ached and his lungs filled. His entire being reacted to this threatening statement and even the big man was moved by the small man's transformation.

"I didn't see you until it was too late. You were going slowly, the car passed me and you, and I didn't see you. You were going too slowly!" Harry shrilly answered, his voice rising and breaking simultaneously. Harry's eyes flashed back a message to the large man that triggered a thought from deep within him. Never had he seen such an intense fear in any man's eyes before.

The injured big man had seen that look before but never in a man's eyes. His mind raced back to when that same look had previously haunted him.

His hounds had treed a raccoon up a relatively small birch tree down by the river in his bottom land. By the time he reached the tree, the raccoon had realized the hopelessness of his situation.

A small tree, six snapping jaws at its' base and the biggest evil of all crashed through the brush heading in his direction. The look in that raccoon's eyes haunted him to this day.

He didn't kill the raccoon; he couldn't. He remembered the considerable effort it took to pull the dogs away from the tree, their almost comical look of puzzlement at leaving that very much alive raccoon up that very small tree.

But he couldn't not after the way it had looked at him. He never revealed that secret to a soul for fear of the chastisement it would have brought upon him from his peers.

The big man saw that look again when his mind returned to the situation at hand. The pain in his leg and shoulder all of a sudden became obvious to him which gave him a perfect excuse to look away from this man who he had every right to be pissed off at.

"Do you have a registration for that tractor? Is it street legal? What about the minimum speed limit? Were your lights on, have you…?" A stern warning look from the big man stopped him at mid-sentence, and he knew he had said enough.

Harry turned away to avoid further antagonizing the man. As it turned out, Harry didn't require any medical care, as he didn't sustain even a scratch from the collision. The state trooper did a thorough examination at the site of the accident and surmised that neither the Datsun nor the tractor was at fault.

The real fault lay with the driver of the Oldsmobile, who recklessly accelerated while passing two vehicles and then slammed on his brakes when realizing that he had miscalculated the distance-to-speed ratio between them and his own car. Unfortunately, that vehicle was long gone and no one caught the tag number.

Ellis, however, did sustain injuries, and an ambulance was called to the scene. Witnesses stated that the driver of the Datsun saw that he was hemmed in and swerved back behind the tractor whereupon he realized that he was rapidly coming up on the back of it.

The driver then swerved the car off the road and into the adjacent ditch to avoid a full collision. The officer surmised that they probably saved the tractor driver's life. No citation tickets were written to the parties involved. He did however get a full description of the Oldsmobile in the chance that it may be spotted.

It wasn't. Ellis was taken to Buncome County General Hospital where X-rays were taken of his leg. Fortunately, there were no broken bones. The road burns down his entire left leg were indeed painful but would heal with proper care and in due time. The officer explained his findings to Ellis and told him that the evasive actions taken by the Datsun may very well have saved his life.

Ellis let that sink in. The only fatality was Miss Nadine's cat whom everyone had been huddled around at the site of the accident. Who was going to break that news to her? She once had stabbed her husband for railing over that cat's tail with his rocking chair.

Chapter Fourteen
Harry Helps Build A Barn
What A Wise Guy

As good a day as any to get started on this, Ellis thought to himself. His leg had healed nicely and he could no longer use it as an excuse to delay the inevitable. I've put it off as long as I could and now I'm flat out of excuses, he said to himself.

The old barn had served him well for over forty-five years but that last summer storm literally had pushed it over the edge. His neighbor Willard Benson owed him a favor and razed the old one for him. Even hauled the debris to a landfill.

Good neighbors like that are hard to come by. That barn had been home to his thirty beef cattle and also stored a year's worth of hay, sericea and lespedesa feed. Luckily, he had a large storage building apart from the barn that he had modified to house the cows until the new structure could be completed.

Now came the fun part. He had to get a building permit that the county now required for anything from hanging a ceiling fan to building a mansion. Such a royal pain in the ass! He didn't know anyone that could draw up the plans for the barn so he went to the local building supply store for help.

Of course, there was a line today; it must be the day everyone is building a new barn. Oh well, what the hell. He made himself as comfortable as he could by shifting his weight on his feet on the hard concrete floor.

"Oh man, this is going to be fun", he said aloud. "Excuse me?" The man ahead of him thought he was talking to him. "I'm sorry. Just thinking out loud." He looked at the man and it slowly dawned on him who the guy was. Oh hell no. Not him, not today. It was the man who had almost killed him on Highway 72 by slamming his car into his tractor.

Harry also recognized Ellis at about that same moment and his heart almost stopped. It's him! What is him doing here? He could not think of a single thing to say to him. He started sweating.

Oh, I know, I'll pretend I don't recognize him. That will work! Finally, he mustered up all of the courage he had and said, "Sir, you can g-get in front of me if you like."

"What good will that do me?" he growled. "It would just shorten the line from seven to six. Just keep your spot." Ellis looked at Harry and thought back to when he had seen that look on Harry's face before.

The fear in his eyes just didn't match the circumstance. He softened a bit. "Look, it's nice of you to offer. Thanks anyway." Harry didn't know what to think. So the man's not going to pull a knife on him and gut him like a pig! Ellis was the next to speak. "What are you here for?"

"The grass in my yard won't grow. No matter how much I water it." I'm trying to get some help." Ellis responded, "I can help with that. I know the soil in this area as good as anyone and better than most. Your soil is too acidic. Put down some lime and water it in. Aerate the yard before you weed and feed the lawn. You should see a big difference."

Harry's head was racing! What? Here is the man I almost killed being nice to me and to top it off he is helping me! There is a God after all! Harry finally spoke" Thank you so much! Here, let me pay you something.

Ellis replied, "Forget it. Glad I could help." Harry took two deep breaths and spoke. "What brings you here?" he boldly charged forward. I'm building a new barn. The old one finally gave out. I've got to have plans and specs to submit to the county to get a building permit". Harry couldn't believe what he was hearing.

He remembered the man's name from the accident police report and responded. "Mr. Hienkle, I can help you with that! That's part of what I do. I'm a Civil Engineering technician. I'd be glad to help you with that", he repeated. Ellis looked at him suspiciously and didn't say a word for two minutes.

Finally, "And you have done this before?" "Numerous times, Harry replied." "Ellis sighed, formed a tight smile and said, "Well, I'll be damned! What did you say your name was, son?" "Harry Campo."

Ellis and Harry agreed to meet the week after the upcoming Saturday or Saturday week as the locals called it. Ellis reminded him that he knew full well where he lived, as it was right in front of the house where Harry had nearly killed him.

Harry showed up in a sports coat with a thin matching tie, denim blue jeans and lace-up shoes. He checked himself out in front of his full-length mirror before he left and had to mentally agree with himself that he looked very professional. Harry arrived right at the agreed upon time.

Ellis was sitting in a chair under an elm tree. When Harry got out of his car, Ellis rolled his eyes. "Harry, you say you've done this before? Son, we are going out into a pasture covered in cow shit." Harry let that sink in and realized that indeed he was overdressed for the occasion. Ellis spoke before Harry could get a word out. "Don't worry; I've got boots that you can put on." And so it began.

Harry indeed knew what he was doing and Ellis relaxed some. They started with the basics, the required dimensions for the lower level as well as the upstairs loft, and then placed the barn relative to the terrain. Ellis stated that placing the barn was the hardest part of the task; if you didn't square the corners correctly, nothing else worked according to plan. Builders in the area used the old 3-4-5 method to place the corners.

On a typical house, it worked OK but a barn was typically wider and longer than a house. If you get off by too much, the barn won't be square and true. You would have to go 3-4-5 on each corner and keep moving the strings on the batter boards to finally get it right. A real pain but it had to be done.

Harry stopped Ellis. "Sir, we won't have to do that. We will get it located correctly the first time." "And how pray tell will we pull off this miracle." "We'll use the Rules of Pythagoras to do this for us."

Ellis wanted to laugh but he could see that Harry was dead serious. "OK Einstein, explain." "The 3-4-5 method is actually a shortcut to the Rules of Pythagoras. Let me sketch our barn. Each side will be 48 feet long. The front and rear will be 30 feet wide.

The dimension we need is the diagonal between them to keep the structure square. The Rules of Pythagoras can provide this with the following equation: 'the square root of A square + B square equals C square'. It's not as complex as it sounds. We know the front of the barn will be 30 feet (30 ft x 30 ft = 900 ft). The sides will be 48 feet (48 ft x48 ft = 2,304 ft). So 900 + 2,304 = 3,204

The square root of 3,204 √ = 56.6 ft; that, sir, is your diagonal dimension.

Now, let me show you why the 3-4-5 method is a shortcut. Let's start with the front right corner of the barn. Going down the side, we will measure out the 4 feet length. Going across the front of the barn, we'll measure across 3 feet.

Now let's measure the diagonal by moving the strings. Now, let's do the math. Front: (3 ft x 3 ft = 9 ft). The side: (4 ft x 4 ft = 16 ft).

So 9 + 16 = 25: Square root √ 25 = 5

"You agree?" "Sure, but that's how we do it now. Nobody knows what that diagonal dimension is going to be, which is why we do 3-4-5. What the hell is a square root?" "It's a number which produces a specified quantity when multiplied by itself." He saw Ellis's eyes glaze over and stopped his explanation. "It's just a name; from now on, we will call it 'the diagonal number maker.' It looks like this on a calculator { √ }."

Now, I want you to do it on this calculator that I'm going to give you.

Front: (3 ft x 3 ft = 9 ft). The side: (4 ft x 4 ft = 16 ft).

So 9 + 16 = 25

Square root √ 25 = 5

9 + 16 = 25. Now, press the'diagonal number' button. What does the screen say?" It's says 5.

Now let's lay out your barn.

Front: (30 ft x 30 ft = 900 ft). The side: (48 ft x 48 ft = 2,304 ft).

So 900 + 2,304 = 3,204

Press the 'diagonal number button { √ }'. What does the screen say? 56.6 ft. That is your diagonal distance."

Ellis whistled under his breath. "Son of a gun! And it works every time?" "Yes sir, every time. What if it's 15 feet wide and 55 feet long? "Yes, it will give you the exact diagonal dimension. Go ahead and do it. "

Front: (15 ft x 15 ft = 225 ft). The side: (55 ft x 55 ft = 3,025 ft).

So 225 + 3,025 = 3,250

"Press the 'diagonal number maker button { √ }'. What's it say? 57.1"

"Son, that is amazing! Did you come up with this?" "No sir. Mr. Pythagoras did over 1,500 years ago." "Wow, pretty smart fellow. Well, you aren't giving me a calculator. I'll buy it from you.

Good grief, so many buttons on this thing. What are those for?" "It does a lot of different calculations. But for the time being let's focus on {√}.

And sir, I've got another calculator; I no longer need this one. This is a Texas Instruments SR50 model. It's as heavy as a brick due to all the transistors, diodes and such that it uses. In recent years, they have improved and miniaturized microprocessors and developed a faster and much lighter model, the SR50A. So please, my gift to you." "Son, you are all right. I'll not forget this."

They both heard the noise of someone walking at a brisk pace towards where they were standing. "Fella, what in the hell are you doing here? You damn near killed him the last time you saw him. Are you coming back to finish the job?"

Willard Jones was Ellis' neighbor who lived a few acres over. Even though they lived some distance apart, they technically did live next door to each other. And yes, he was a bit nosey. "Ease off a little, Willard. I invited him over. He's helping me with the new barn." OK, I didn't know. Wait, what?" was his genuine reply of disbelief.

"How in the world can this guy help you raise a barn? My wife is stockier than this chap!" Ellis commenced to explain Mr. Pythagorus to Willard, who remained skeptical of the entire concept. "Sounds like so much big talk. I don't like the name Pythagoras either. Sounds subversive. My Staff Sergeant over in Korea had almost the exact same last name. And to tell you the truth, I never trusted him either." Harry spoke without thinking.

"You fought in the Korean War? So did my Dad." Willard looked at him, really looked at him for the first time since he walked over. "Oh he did, did he? What branch of service?"

"He was in the Army 34th Infantry operating out of the 24th Infantry Division. He was there for over a year when he got shot. I was quite young, so I don't remember all of the particulars. I do remember he was hospitalized for quite a while as the two bullets tore him up pretty badly. '7.62 by 54'.

That was the bullet size that hit him fired from a Mosin Nagant rifle. I do remember hearing that being said quite often." Willard softened a bit. "I'm sorry to hear that, son." There was an uncomfortable silence that hung in the air for a while. Finally, Ellis spoke, "Harry showed me a much better way to square up the corners of the barn; way better than using the 3-4-5 method. Even gave me a calculator to ensure that the dimensions were entered correctly."

"Really?" He was genuinely interested. "Can you show me how to do that?" Harry replied, "I sure can. Better yet Ellis, you show him." At first, Ellis objected but then thought that really did make sense. "OK, sure. He used a 25' long by 20' wide dwelling. He entered the data and pressed the Diagonal Dimension button. 32.01'. Willard whistled between his teeth. "And 32.01' is the correct diagonal length?" "Yes, it is. And it works every time?" "Every time." "Well, now, that is worth knowing. That's real helpful son. Real helpful. Much obliged. Where can I get one of those calculators?"

"I might get you one for nothing. Everyone in my office has switched from the TI SR50 to the TI SR50A. I'll ask around.' "Oh no, I'll pay for it. That is real helpful, son. Real helpful."

Ellis chimed in. "Let's go back to the house. I want to introduce you to my wife." Harry agreed, feeling on top of the world.

Chapter Fifteen

Old Resident: Ellis Heinkle's Wife

Clara, Rn Rural Nurse

"Clara, you have said enough! Enough!" By saying that, all Ellis had served to do was piss her off. The introduction had gone smoothly; she liked Harry straight away. The homemade scuppernong wine she served was making her chatty and she was in the mood to talk. "Harry, when I was young, I was a big help to Doctor Arbolt. He was always busy 'cause he was the only game in town. In school, I wasn't a good student.

I just wasn't that interested in the A B Cs; school bored me and my grades reflected it. "Clara, please. You've said enough. I mean it now. Enough." Ellis was looking at his watch; his dental appointment was coming up fast and he had to come up with a creative way to get Harry out of the place before he had to leave.

Wine always went through Clara quickly because she seldom if ever drank the stuff. But when she did, oh what a chatterbox. "Clara, Harry needs to be on his way. Harry, we'll talk later." Harry sensed the tension between the two of them and wanted to go even though he was very curious about what Clara wanted to tell him.

"I do have things to do; it would be best that I leave now" Harry replied, not wanting to make matters worse. "Thanks again for the wine. It was really good." Ellis breathed a sigh of relief and headed for the door. He was running late and knew he would be late for his appointment.

Harry grabbed up his coat and notebook and headed for the door. Clara stopped Harry when she knew Ellis was out of earshot. "Harry, wait. Let me get you a bottle of that wine to take home with you." She wouldn't listen to his objections; she insisted that he take one with him.

"We've got over a hundred bottles; we won't miss one. I am the one who learned to make wine and do you know who taught me? Doctor Arbolt, that's who. "He gave me a fermenter bucket, gave me chemicals to sanitize everything. I remember the name of it 'cause I liked to say it. Potassium metabysulfite.

Also gave me a five-gallon glass jug he called a Carboy. I always like saying that word too. Carboy. We didn't need to add store bought yeast to ferment the grapes; natural yeast did that for us. You'd take a big balloon and stretch it over the neck of the Carboy. Carboy. Don't you like that word?" Harry had to honestly admit he did. The name didn't fit the circumstance at all.

"Yes Ma'am, that is a good word. "I got really good at making wine. It was hard work but it was fun to me. When it started to ferment, the gas swelled the balloon. By the way, making any wine comes down to this simple fact. The yeast eats sugar and grapes are full of sugar. The yeast eats the sugar and as it does it pisses alcohol and farts carbon dioxide gas. She laughed. Doesn't sound so fancy when you say it like that but it's every word true. After four or five weeks, the balloon would deflate letting you know it was getting ready. Don't rush it too much though.

If there is still sugar in the wine, it may continue fermenting after you bottle it. That happened to me once. You talk about a mess. On my first attempt at winemaking, I bottled it too early and the yeast was still hungry, happily pissing alcohol and farting gas into a screw-top bottle. That gas pressure got so high it burst that bottle. Went off like a .22 rifle shot.

Ellis thought it was a rifle shot and ran into the bedroom to get his side-by-side double barrel 20 gauge shotgun. It didn't take long to figure out what happened. The shattered bottle was in the pantry along with a river of wine all over the floor. It took hours to clean up that mess. Only happened that one time.

My Daddy used to say that was not a mistake, that was a blunder, and you never repeat a blunder." Harry was fascinated so Clara continued.

"So anyway, Doctor Arbolt always said, if it was any kind of plant, he could do something with it. Did you know he could make wine from dandelions? He could and it was good. He could take a weed and make it delicious.

Back then, medicines were sometimes in short supply. So the good doctor would gather up various plants and use them to treat ailments.

I was fascinated by knowing that and wanted to know more. I talked his ear off, asking him questions about everything. He told my daddy, 'She asks me every question that could be asked and then asks it twice'. And he was right; I would. He taught me how different plants cured different conditions and I learned quickly.

My brain was like a sponge. I worked up all my courage and asked Daddy if I could ride along with Doctor Arbolt when he made his rounds. I hadn't even asked Doctor Arbolt yet! I told Daddy I would be useful and not get in the way.

He was just thrilled that I was going to be good at something. My grades at school never amounted to much. Daddy approached Doctor Arbolt about it and believed it or not, he was 'receptive to the idea'. And so it started.

On my first ride with him, our first stop was the Robinson family. Mr. Robinson always had high blood pressure. He gave him sasparilla tea, which controlled it quite well. It tasted like root beer because it is the base ingredient of root beer.

He mostly used sassafra root to make that tonic. Tea was his favorite way to provide medicine. He preferred to serve it without sugar, but sometimes, there was no other way to ingest it. But he would always tell them to try it unsweetened first.

I remember a lady named Helen Howards. She suffered from arthritis, something awful. I would dig up the roots of a ginseng plant, and Doctor Arbolt would boil them down to make a poultice out of it. He would apply that poultice directly on the aching joints and it drew out the pain.

Oh Lord. I remember James McDowell. The man was always constipated. Doc would make a tea out of senna leaves mixed with two teaspoons of turpentine and it would open the man's plugged bowel. But, oh, the noise! And what a smell! This won't come as a shock; he also suffered from hemorrhoids.

Doc would take a teaspoon of alum and mix it in a pint jar of hog's lard to make a salve. He would let Mister McDowell apply it to the hemorrhoids himself for obvious reasons.

"The worst case of poison ivy I ever saw was Willard Benson. They were clearing an area that bordered the bottom land at the creek at the back of his property. They knew the poison ivy was there, so they took what they thought was the necessary precautions to keep from getting it.

A couple of days later, he had blisters on his ankles and wrists that showed where the larger vines had contacted his skin. A few days later, it was all over him. The poor man was in agony.

Doctor Arbolt was on the other side of the county so it was up to me. It was my first real opportunity to be a doctor. I knew what to do; I had watched the good doctor treat folks many times. We made up a tub of water, made it as hot as Willard could stand it and added a generous amount of table salt to it.

He soaked it for one hour in it. We tried to keep the bath water temperature consistent by pouring in a ladle of hot water as needed. His wife handled that part of the treatment. I wouldn't have minded doing it; he was a handsome thing!

Anyway, when that part of the treatment was over we applied Vaseline to the affected area of his body. Again, his wife did that. I offered to do it but she said no. Oh well, win some lose some."

There was Agnes Harper. She had twisted her left ankle years ago and from time to time, it would swell for no apparent reason. He would make a tea from meadowsweet roses. Drinking that helped her so much. I learned later that the base for aspirin was derived from that same exact flower.

"He pointed out what each plant looked like as we would ride along. At times, he would draw them up on a writing tablet. In truth, his drawings were excellent like something you would see in a textbook. He gave them to me; I still have them.

They are around here somewhere. Sometimes, he would send me out to gather plants on my own. Sometimes he only wanted the leaves, sometimes the whole plant, sometimes just the root. I remember one of those projects particularly well. I was peeling the bark of the base of a sassafra tree focusing only on the bark.

Little did I know there was also a yellow jacket nest at the base of that tree and they were not at all pleased to have me around. I got stung 15 times and boy did that hurt! Yellow jackets are ground dwelling wasps, so unlike a bee they can sting you until they get tired of stinging you.

A honey bee stings you once. Then the stinger pulls out along with a section of the bee's abdomen. They then fly off and die. Now, you are probably wondering did I know how to treat a yellow jacket sting? Right? The answer, of course, I did. I took five or six plantain leaves and made a poultice out of them, then brushed the poultice onto the 15 stings and tied a damp cloth to cover the area. So help me, it did take the stinging sensation as well as the swelling right out.

'Look, I'm talking your ear off. I'm sorry; I enjoy talking about those days". "Don't be sorry!" Harry replied. He was genuinely fascinated.

"Well, that's enough for today. It won't be long until Ellis gets back. It would be best if you weren't still here. It has nothing to do with you; it's just that he's afraid I will talk to you about Red Ivy Tea."

"Red Ivy Tea? You didn't mention that tea. What makes it so special?" "Next time, Harry. Next time. You better go." They agreed that Harry should return on Saturday week.

"Harry, I appreciate you drawing up the plans for the barn." Ellis said to him when Saturday week rolled around. "Willard is going to need plans for the storage building with side sheds we're going to build for him in six months.

Be sure to charge him two times the going rate to include my finder's fee." "Well, of course. That seems more than fair," Harry replied with a smile. Clara waved him down. "Harry, that fancy calculator you got for Ellis, does it convert recipe temperatures from metric to something I can understand?"

Harry smiled and nodded to her. "You young man are proving to be a very helpful fellow." He thought about that for a minute, let it sink in and then smiled. "Just glad I could help. What are you cooking up; maybe some of that Red Ivy Tea?" She stared at him for so long that he started to get nervous. Isn't that just like me? He thought to himself. Finally feeling accepted, even needed and then screwed it all up within the next five minutes.

"Clara, I'm sorry, I was just trying to be funny. That happens to me every time I try to tell a joke. That same exact look. You would think I would learn." Clara stopped him mid-sentence.

"No, no Harry you didn't offend. Just the opposite. I couldn't believe you remembered my mentioning that to you; it was from a long time back. If you're not in a hurry, I'll tell you a little more about it if you are interested. By the way, I have some freshly squeezed lemonade chilling in the refrigerator."

Harry was genuinely relieved that he hadn't offended her and would have agreed to pay close attention to her teaching him how to boil water. She led the way back to the house.

She put ice cubes in two tumblers and filled them with the lemonade adding a small sprig of fresh mint to the side of each glass. He took a good mouthful. "Clara, this is absolutely delicious. Thank you."

She looked at him and smiled. "Harry, my Daddy would have loved you. When I was a young girl, he cautioned me about the type of man I should look for as 'husband material'. He told me to steer clear of the pretty boys, as they have no eyes for anyone but themselves. Also, the ones quick to anger will at some point in time turn that anger onto you. Also, stay away from loud-talking know-it-alls as you will soon find out that they have nothing to say and know nothing at all. Find yourself a quiet even tempered man with a head full of smarts and you will live a happy life. Yes, he would have loved you."

Harry let that sink in for a while and then smiled. "Your Dad sounds like he gave wise counsel. I wish he was here as I could use some of that good advice right about now. Most women my age don't find the qualities you described as very desirable, especially if that man can't tell a joke.

They tell me that telling a joke comes down to good timing. But here's what I deliver: tiimming, tiemming, TIEming. Get it? She didn't get it. "Well, maybe being a comedian isn't your calling, Harry but you obviously have God given talents. You are helping a lot of us around here with the things that you can deliver and we are grateful. I mean that people talk".

"Now, let me ask you. Are you looking for a wife because I could help you with that." Harry's face got beet red and he stammered. "Well, um I well um uh."

"My goodness son, you are shy aren't you? Let's start a little slower. Would you be interested in some female companionship?" Harry exhaled. "Well, yes. That would be nice."

"All right then, let's start there. Let me ask you a few questions. What matters more to you? What does she believe in or what does she look like?" He laughed. It's as simple as that?"

"'Sometimes it is. Anyway, it's a good place to begin." And so, with that, they began.

For the next two hours, they dug into the far recesses of Harry's mind. Some answers came out easily and some had to be dragged out. Some thoughts were disturbing, some were confusing, and some were even surprising. Clara was non-judgmental through it all. She knew when to be understanding and when to correct. At times, she was sympathetic, completely on his side.

Oh my God, I'm looking for a young version of Clara, he thought to himself. "Harry, I have enough to go on so let me work on this." "OK. Do you think I am 100% crazy he asked with some trepidation? "

"To the contrary, Harry, I think you are 100% normal." Harry beamed a big smile in spite of himself and thought that he was madly in love with her. "So, are you going to mix me up with a love tonic?" She winked at him. "We'll see." But Harry, just remember that loving someone takes on many forms and comes with much responsibility over a person's life. Even expressing that love may look unusual to some, but if you love that person, you do what is needed regardless of what others may think.

"All right now, Harry. Let's get back to the task at hand. I need to speak candidly with you about a sensitive subject. Is that OK with you?" Harry nodded in the affirmative, and Clara began. "Speaking of tonics, one of my tasks for Doctor Arbolt used to involve making Red Ivy Tea. Harry sat up and leaned in a bit.

"I wondered about that. I have never heard that term before. If it is anything like your lemonade, it must taste heavenly." Clara spit a mouthful of lemonade across the table in response and then tried to stifle a laugh. Harry sat there wide-eyed, not knowing what to make of what had just occurred.

"Harry, this is going to take some time to explain. Do you have anything you need to do?" He assured her that he did not but had already decided he would cancel them if he did. She began, Harry, this entire region of the state, from the Piedmont foothills to the mountains was relatively rural until recently. Many of the modern comforts and improvements that we enjoy and take for granted today were simply not available.

As such, we learned to be self-sufficient, make do and live off the land. Neighbors had to help neighbors as a matter of necessity. That also included medical care. Sure, there were hospitals here and there, but in truth, we didn't use them unless it was absolutely necessary.

We had one doctor, Doctor Arbolt, who came to you when needed and covered most of the region I just described. He was very good at some things, pretty good at a few other things and absolutely terrible at others. We made our own medicines, usually from plant roots, vines and leaves.

It's not as farfetched as you might think. If you look up the active ingredients in aspirin, you'll find out they are, in some capacity, extracted from plants. Well, anyway, as people age, the body breaks down and starts preparing for death.

Unfortunately, pain is usually a part of that process. Some passed relatively peacefully; others not so much. For some, they seemed to need the approval to die from family before they would let go. Others just had a 'fighting spirit' and resisted death. And some, for whatever reason, just lingered in agony.

Those were the worst. Sometimes, the pain was excruciating; it was hard to watch. Over the years, our forefathers learned how to help ease that agony and developed an elixir that came to be called Red Ivy Tea. It was a mixture of various roots, the sap of certain trees, some bark, some ivy vines and some ivy leaves.

All would be thoroughly dried, ground down to a powder, heated with a certain liquid that I will not name, and then boiled down the mixture to concentrate it. It was then allowed to sit up overnight.

When it was decided that the only thing left of the dying person was the 'shell' of the body, tea-time had come. The mixture was given by mouth; death usually followed within an hour.

"Stop! What? Stop!" Harry was trembling; he thought he was going to pass out. "You are talking about killing a man. Oh my

God!" He had to stand up and walk around the room. Clara stopped talking. Finally, she smiled at Harry.

"Come sit down, Harry. I know this is difficult to hear, but please understand that nothing else could be done. I want you to take one thing with you about what I have just described. The dying person had no chance of survival, and that person was in agony. Morphine was in scarce supply, and even when we could get it, a normal dose was provided every four hours, and that would wear off every two-three hours and then the moaning, sometimes screaming, would resume.

Where did I fit in with this? I gathered the ingredients, dried them and made the tea. At times, if the doctor just couldn't get there, I served the tea. Harry couldn't hear anything at all at this point. Here, I thought I was going to get her recipe for making delicious lemonade. He started crying. After a few minutes, he pulled himself together.

"Clara, I'm not judging you; hell, I don't judge anybody. It's just not my nature." Harry was still shaken up. She replied, "I know that. I could sense it about you. Why do you think that I wanted to share this part of my history with you? Let me also share this. Throughout history, only one person at a time had the recipe for Red Ivy Tea.

The holder of the recipe would select one person that he trusted and then entrust that person with the recipe. Only one person; at least, that was what Doctor Arbolt told me. Why just one person? If it became common knowledge, people would start using it to kill off people they didn't like.

That was the fear, anyway. Doctor Arbolt passed me the recipe for Red Ivy Tea before he died. He made me promise that I was not to pass the recipe to anyone going forward. He felt that pain management was much better now, and as such, there was no longer a need for it. He and I prayed together, and then I vowed to take the recipe to the grave with me.

But Harry, I still had feelings about it; I wanted to share the story with someone I trusted. I know we haven't known each other long, but when I first met you, I thought of my Daddy's words. I knew you were the one to share my story. She stopped talking then, as she knew she had said enough.

Harry just sat there for several minutes.

Finally, he cleared his throat. "Clara that must have been hard at first. To come to the decision to serve the tea. I know a little about what pain looks like. When I was a young boy, my Dad died from complications from gunshot wounds he got in the Korean War. He lingered for so long. I was too young to fully understand all that was going on but I do remember when he took a turn for the worse. That was the last time I didn't get to see him. They thought I was too young to understand what was going on. One more time, though, would have been nice. He called me his little angel. I am honored that you selected me to share this story. I promise I will not share it."

One question, "Why do you feel the need to tell this story now?" He had already sensed the reason but wanted to hear her say it. Clara smiled, "Your poker face isn't too good. Another reason for you not to take up gambling. So there you have it: don't do standup comedy, and don't gamble. Is it a deal"? He smiled and nodded his head.

"Harry, they have found a tumor on my left breast and neighboring lymph nodes. They feel that they have caught it early enough, so the prognosis is pretty good. But one never knows. I think you have heard enough for one day, don't you?" He exhaled and laughed out loud.

"Ah yea, I think so. "Here's a quart Mason jar of lemonade to take with you. Harry then did something that surprised even him. He kissed Clara on the cheek. "All right, son. Get on out of here. I've got floors to mop," she said with a twinkle in her eye. After a few minutes, Ellis asked her through the window, "Is it safe to come in?" "Yep, he's gone. Come on in".

Chapter Sixteen

New Resident Will Ziefer
Friend of Wernher Von Braun

"How does Harry Campo do it? It defies conventional wisdom." All agreed. "Our lawns look like they have experienced a drought, and his looks like an oasis in our desert. It just doesn't make sense. I've tried to talk to him about it when he drives by, but he just looks at me, nods his head my way and steps on the gas. He is a bit of an odd duck. Having said that, I have seen him at Robert's Esso gas station laughing it up with the locals. What gives? That being said, I would like to know what he is doing that we aren't".

"Speaking of odd ducks, have any of you talked with Will Ziefer? He and his wife live in the third house on the right on Endive Drive. He's an older fellow, kind of quiet, and keeps to himself. He told me he was an engineer. I invited him over to drink a beer last week. He's a nice enough sort. Well, one beer led to four, and he got pretty chatty. What a story he told me! He said the Americans brought him over to the USA against his wishes towards the end of World War II, along with Wernher Von Braun and 1,200 other German engineers to help with rocket and missile development.

Back in Germany, he told me he had worked closely with Wernher on the development of the V2 rocket, among other things and told me 'he was damn good' at it". The Americans lagged in this technology, and so as part of war reparations, they selected and moved him along with other engineers, scientists and technicians to the USA. They designed and worked on rockets at top-secret bases in California and, of all places, in Alabama. The success of the Saturn rocket used to fly men in the Apollo spacecraft to the moon and back was largely due to this team of German engineers. They could not go anywhere without a military escort. They called themselves POPs – Prisoners of Peace since we were no longer at war at that time.

When it was no longer beneficial to keep the group together as a cohesive team they broke them up and placed them individually into small towns all over the USA to help with machine design in many different industries. Every effort was made to ensure that the locals did not know who they were or the critical help they had already provided to our country.

There was always an overseer in these towns to ensure they were treated well by the locals and monitor the Germans' comings and goings. He himself was first assigned to a small town right here in North Carolina, where he worked for a company that built industrial washing machines which he pointed out was a far cry from building rockets and missiles. Rocket engineers making industrial washing machines. Having said that, his team made many improvements to the machines.

He laughed when he told me that the advances they had made in complex venturi designs as a critical part of rocket propulsion lent itself to the process of moving fabric through an industrial washer with minimal contact with the machine itself. This was in the early 1960's polyester fiber was in big demand at that time. After it was woven into a fabric, it required little to no ironing. But it had two flaws. Every time the fabric touched any pulley, reel or guide inside the washing machine, it would develop a sheen finish to it. Even worse, it would create hundreds of small yarn 'pills' made up of broken filaments across the fabric caused by contact with those pulleys, reels and guides during the washing process. The washing process had to be performed under pressure to create a consistent, thorough cleaning, which added to the stress on the fabric.

His team designed an adjustable venturi that would create a pressure variation, with higher pressure in the throat of the venturi and lower pressure exiting, which caused the fabric passing through it to be gently "pulled" due to this difference in pressure. The liquid in the machine protected the fabric, causing little direct contact with the machine itself. The finished fabric was beautiful, with no sheen and no pilling. That company immediately applied for patents around the globe and sold hundreds of them.

He enjoyed living in the USA and worked hard to fit in. Most did not know how or why he ended up there, and not wanting to appear rude, essentially never asked him about his history. He remembered when he was still in Alabama that, a few local men he worked with had invited him and his wife to the American Legion dance held every Friday night. One did ask him, "You were in the military, weren't you?" Before he had time to think about it, he blurted out, "Yes, in the Luftwaffe." Funny thing, he was never invited to future dances.

While he enjoyed living here, he always longed to go back home to Germany. His wife did not share his enthusiasm and vowed never to go back there. She was a young girl living in Dresden prior to Germany surrendering. From time to time, she still had screaming nightmares about the firestorms that she had witnessed as a young girl caused by carpet bombing by the Allied forces.

"His favorite novel of all time was 'The Three Kingdoms'. Wait a second. Yes, here it is. He wrote the name of the book and its' author on a piece of paper for me. It's in my wallet; yes, here it is".

He absolutely did not trust the communist regime in China. "Neighbor, China is always plotting, always planning. Do yourself and others a favor and read the Chinese novel 'The Three Kingdoms' by Luo Guanzhong. It's been recently translated into English. There is an old Chinese saying, 'If you read The Three Kingdoms three times, I cannot do business with you. You would know my strategies, understand my thinking and perhaps use my schemes against me.'

"I could see by the look on Will's face that he saw serious doubts in my eyes. He stood up, took a faded photograph out of his wallet and showed me a picture of him and Wernher. He smiled, finished his beer in one big gulp and said, "Auf wiedersehen, nachbar."

Chapter Seventeen
Saturday Afternoon in Paradise.
Where Is Burt Reynolds When You Need Him?

In gathering numbers, people from the neighborhood started making their way towards the Harristons' split level along with the kids and a picnic basket full of assorted homemade or at least home-warmed goodies.

It was a perfect day for a cookout with a cool breeze coming off the lake located to the west of the subdivision. The eastern breezes weren't nearly as welcomed as they invariably came off and over Mr. Heinkel's cow pastures. But today, things couldn't be better. These get-togethers had been Ellen Harriston's idea a few months back and everyone always seemed to enjoy themselves. Ellen was waiting at the gate by the side of the house as she patiently watched the neighborhood converge on her backyard.

"Patty, for goodness sake, you didn't need to bring another basketful of food this week. You brought enough last week to feed everybody here, so quit showing off. We all know that you can cook now, so quit showing off."

Patty laughed and replied "Don't worry; there's no food in here this time. While I keep you occupied, Jack is going to sneak into your house and steal your sterling flatware."

Ellen feigned shock and then barred the gate entrance with her arms. "Oh, Ellen, don't pay Patty any attention at all. She has always got a cute remark for everything. Besides, I've seen your sterling. It's all silver plate."

Ellen laughed and looked truly shocked at Jack's remark. She punched him lightly on his shoulder as he walked by and then held onto his arm for support as she took the basket from him. She supported herself longer than she needed to, and Patty sensed it. Jack sensed it too, but neither said a word. Within thirty minutes, there was a total of twenty-six people in the Harristons' backyard, with four barbeque grills turning out half-cooked hamburgers and hot dogs at an alarming rate. The condiments on the three fold out tables included both sweet and sour slaw, chili, chips, relishes, homemade dip made with Velveeta cheese, halved hard-boiled eggs worked over with salad dressing topped with smoked paprika as well as homemade apple pies bought fresh at the supermarket. There was Kool-Aid for the kiddies, Gator-Aid for the teens, Seven-Up for the Un-cola crowd and Coors Lite for those looking to keep the calories down. Everyone else got Pepsi.

There were swings for the young kids, a basketball goal for the older kids, and a sports channel on a nineteen-inch color set on the deck behind the house for the men. The women had chaise lounge chairs under the trees so they could talk and watch the kids at the same time.

The teenagers bragged about what sex was like, the women talked about what sex should be, and the men talked about the LA Raiders until the cheerleaders came on the screen. Then, the men talked about sex with a Raiderette. In truth, everyone there had a grand time. Meeting with the neighbors cultivated a sense of unity and a feeling of genuine companionship and tended to make everyone forget their problems for a while. Everyone there knew that the gatherings wouldn't last long.

"Patty, why did you and Jack have only one child?" Samantha asked between bites of corn chips. She normally wouldn't have been so open to someone she had only known for two months on a part-time basis, but a couple of beers had that kind of effect on her. Patty thought a minute for a proper answer when Ellen beat her to it. "Shoot, Samantha, why did you have five? Couldn't you and Bill think of anything else to do in your spare time?" Samantha nearly spits half a mouthful of corn chips all over to group but manages to catch most of it in her hand.

"Well, my God, it beats taking up needlepoint," she replied while wiping herself off with a napkin. Ellen was ready. "Well, I'll grant you that, but at least I give my needle a rest every now and then." The whole group exploded into laughter which caused every head in the back yard to turn in their direction. When the men realized that no one was choking, they turned back to their ball game.

Bill turned to the others and grinned. "With that much laughing, the women must be talking about one of our sex lives. "Well, it sure as hell ain't mine. Patty doesn't even talk about our sex life with me," Jack stated without even taking his eyes off the television. "Now, Jack, don't even try to tell me that the honeymoons' already over with that gorgeous woman you are married to. Man, that woman's got it all going on." Jack truly thought about what he had just said and then shook his head.

"Listen, I know it. I'm just blowing smoke. Yeah, Patty is an amazing lady. Better than I deserve." He squirmed and looked for a way to change topics. Paul was having no part of that and the beer started talking. "My friend, you have a baby doll. If that was my wife, I'd have her locked up while I was at work. Better yet, I'd quit work." Jack seriously wanted the conversation to end. "Look, I know what I've got. I was trying to be funny. "Besides, Paul. Gloria's not a bad-looking woman herself if you are truly looking for an excuse to quit work." A few of them on the deck snickered.

"Gloria? Lord, man. There's a hell of a difference between looking good and being good if you get my drift. Her idea of being sexy is coming to bed in pajamas with feet in them. She likes it one way. Once a month on the first Sunday morning before church with the lights off. Once, I asked her to go down on me. She slapped me so hard I had to get two fillings reset. I figured visual aids would help, so I brought home a porno movie. Even rented a videocassette recorder. She watched the movie for about two minutes and then got up and packed her bags. I mean, she went home to momma! And I don't mean this happened ten years ago. This was eight months ago!

The beer was really kicking in. She told her momma the works; the blow job, the movie, the whole nine yards. That woman only had sex one time in her life. And said she wouldn't have then had it not been for her old man threatening to leave her. After all, they had been married for five years. To this day, that woman will barely speak to me. She calls me 'that pervert' even in front of the kids.

She told Gloria not to leave me alone with my own daughter. Yes, sir, that woman is a real angel!' Everybody on the deck was grinning like mules eating briars by this time, even Jack. Walter asked, "Well, Bill, we all now know not to bother you on the first Sunday morning of the month, but what do you do every other day of the week?" "What do I do? I'll tell you what I do. I fuck out; that's what I do. There is this little twenty-five-year-old clerk at work who asked ME out. Knowing I was married and everything. Can you believe that? She asked me out! We met at the Bar Pomodora at the Asheville Hilton and had a few drinks to loosen ME up. She later told me then we got a room. It was unbelievable.

Before we got started, she told me not to be afraid to tell her how I wanted it. She told me that she had heard that in a Burt Reynolds movie so she figured that guys liked to hear it. I nearly had a baby! I hollered as loud as I could. THANK YOU, BURT! The whole group went into hysterics. Every head in the backyard turned their way. When the women realized that no one was choking, they continued.

"Well, Samantha, Jack and I really couldn't afford more than one, that's all. We still practice, though." "I'll bet you do, Ellen interjected. Samantha broke in. "Do any of you ever have fantasies about other men when you're, you know, doing it?" "Doing what, Samantha?" Ellen asked. Baking cookies, you dummy. Ellen looked at her in total disbelief.

"Well, I'm forty, uh, well, approaching middle age, and I've never heard it called that before. Baking cookies?" Samantha turned red. "You know what I'm talking about, oh, forget it." Ellen smiled at her with her eyes and finished the sentence for her. "Sure, Sam, I do it all the time. I mean after three husbands and none of them turning out to be knights in shining armor, I tend to make up my knights to help me through the nights. Doesn't everybody?"

Everybody agreed, some more reluctantly than others. "That's not to say I'd cheat on Bill unless he was really good-looking. Like that Harry, what's his name?" Patty spoke up, "Oh, be still my heart.

The whole group giggled and then felt strangely remorseful for doing so. "Patty, you ought to be ashamed. Poor Harry can't help the way he is. Still, can you imagine what it would be like with him?

You would have to help him through the whole thing and do it without offending him or hurting his feelings, "Ellen stated.

The beer had really loosened Patty up. " Yeah, it would be quite the experience. Please Harry, touch me here, now there. Not like that, open your fists." The women screamed. Samantha rolled out of her chair laughing. Every head in the backyard paid them absolutely no attention at all. They all knew that no one was choking.

Chapter Eighteen
Neighbor Helping Neighbor
What Would the World Do Without Harry

The incessant ringing of his doorbell finally shook Harry from a deep sleep that he really didn't want to end. He laid there silently; hoping whoever was out there would just go away. He soon realized the rude person out there was stronger-willed than he was because he refused to leave. Nobody ever rang his doorbell, so why is it that on the one day, he really needed the sleep, he somehow became the most popular guy in the subdivision?

Oh, what the hell. Harry opened the door and, through squinted eyes, slowly brought the person into focus. James Hamilton from two houses down. "Hi Harry, hope this isn't a bad time". Harry wanted to tell him it was the worst possible time. I just learned how to kill someone. Are you sure you want to bother me NOW? Of course, he didn't say anything like that. Instead, he said, "No, its fine. What can I do to help you?"

James went on to explain that the whole neighborhood wanted to know his secret to creating a beautiful lawn. "Our yards look like they are the desert to your oasis. How do you do it? I'll pay you to show me what to do to achieve those results." Harry stated, "Well, to start, you have to stay away from Indian grass. That will create a patchy yard".

"OK, got that. Don't plant Indian grass. What else?" "What I meant, oh good grief. Clara, you are so right. I must stay away from comedy". James was thoroughly confused. "So, then what?" Harry stopped him. "I'm sorry; it's been a pretty heavy day. Here is what you need to do. The soil is too acidic; you need to neutralize it with lime. You can buy it at any hardware store. Also, there's a county man named Adam Delmar who will come out and take samples of your soil and send them to Raleigh in order to analyze them further. It doesn't cost a thing to have that done."

James looked at him in wide-eyed amazement. Finally, he cleared his throat. "Thank you so much! You really have done your homework. Would you mind if I came by again with any questions?" "Sure, I'll be glad to help if I can." "What do I owe you? Harry thought a minute and replied, "How about one million dollars? Just kidding. It has been pointed out to me very recently that I am no Tommy Smothers. I'll leave the jokes to other folks. You don't owe me a thing." "Harry, we are going to have a block party at my place next Saturday. Starts at 12:00 noon, and we would love to have you. Just come on over. Don't bring anything except a healthy appetite." "OK, thanks. I'll be there." And for the first time in his life, he meant it. And for the first time in his life, he went.

The turnout for the backyard soiree was good. Even better than the previous one. Harry almost backed out at the last minute but then thought the better of it. He said a quick prayer which did settle his nerves some.

About that time, James spotted his arrival and walked out to warmly greet him which surprised everyone there. "Harry, glad you could make it. Let me introduce you to this motley crew. A few stammered some stood with their mouths gaping open, and one asked if he had somehow stepped through a time warp. Finally, James cleared up the confusion.

Everyone, this is your neighbor, Harry Campo. He has been helping me with my lawn, a lawn that, as all can see, is in desperate need of attention. I have come to the conclusion he is a genius in this 'field', get it?" Everyone got it and laughed.

Harry smiled and thought to himself, unbelievable. "We are just getting started with mine, but one has only to look at his yard to see what we hope to achieve. His first advice to me is don't plant Indian grass; it will produce a patchy lawn. The group roared with laughter.

"Seriously, he said that. I love his sense of humor. Come on, let's make him feel welcome." Folks surrounded him, some with hands extended, some patting him on the back. Harry thought to himself, have '**I**' walked through a time warp? He was given business cards from several people, all inviting him over, and all wanting a lawn makeover. Harry was gracious to all and agreed to help them all, which made him pause. He realized that the friendships he was creating with the local folks were having some kind of profound effect on him.

It dawned on him the locals were sincere, genuine people without ulterior motives and little to no pretensions. In other words, they genuinely liked him, and he genuinely liked them. This was starting to spill over into other aspects of his life. Harry was starting to realize that he had always tended to focus inward as a defense mechanism. The problem with that; he didn't like what he saw. That would depress him, which, of course, would make him focus inward all the more. It would also make him search out the bad in others to offset the negative feelings about himself. Was that a cybernetic loop or a Catch-22? Regardless, it had defined most of his life.

The last couple that Harry met was Jack and Patty Owens. They seemed nice, if a little distracted. He was not surprised when Jack mentioned that they needed help with their lawn; it was very obvious that they did. Jack started detailing the things they had already tried with limited success when Patty stopped him.

"Jack, we agreed that my Grandpa was going to help us when he got back on his feet. He is really good with this kind of thing." "Yeah, Patty, I know. And you are right; he is. Maybe Harry can kind of give us a head start on it; that's all." Patty stared at both of them as tears welled up in her eyes before turning and walking away.

There was complete silence for a minute. Jack cleared his throat. Harry was the first to speak.

"Listen, if I said something to hurt her feelings, I am genuinely sorry. I have been known to say the wrong thing at the wrong time. If that is the case here, let me go and apologize."

"Harry, I wish it was as simple as that. See, Patty adores her Granddad always has. She was the apple of his eye going all the way back to when she was a little girl. He was always a strong, robust man. Well, he now has bone cancer, which has metastasized into his brain. Patty refuses to believe a word of his prognosis even though it is painfully obvious to see how fast he is fading. For the last six months, I have walked on eggshells around her. Her Granddad has one request; no, not a request, a demand. He wants to die at home, not in an extended care facility. He has said this statement to every single person who comes to see him: "If you try to put me in a nursing home for me to die in, I pray that the vehicle taking me there will be in an accident that kills me." He is dead ser.., no I mean very serious. He is now in a great deal of pain. But he is a fighter, so you never know how bad the pain is. So stoic. To be honest, I am going to miss him too. He is the sweetest-natured man that would do anything for anybody. His eyes teared up in spite of himself. Harry, without thinking about it, hugged him.

Chapter Nineteen

Patty's Grandpa - Beyond the Sunset

Patty's grandpa, indeed, was a stoic man, one who could seemingly tolerate a considerable amount of pain. As the cancer progressed, even after he suffered a minor stroke, which put him in this hospital, he gave no indication that he was in pain.

Even after he went blind in one eye, there was still no indication that he was in pain. The doctor and nurses on duty at the hospital KNEW he was in pain; they had overseen this condition numerous times, and they were well-versed in pain management. He declined anything stronger than ibuprofen or acetaminophen. It was as if he wanted to stay lucid regardless of the pain.

Sometimes, when he was sleeping, he would moan, sometimes quite loud, but then drift off to sleep. This had been going on for seven weeks and showed no signs of abating. The doctor talked with the family and suggested they put him on a four-hour regimen of morphine. He had thought that they might attempt that and made it abundantly clear that he did not want that. So, what do you do?

He always perked up whenever Patty came to see him which was fairly often. He would smile broader and speak louder when she was there, even though it was obvious to everyone that it took considerable effort on his part. The medical staff knew what had to be done; they had seen it many times before.

When the time came, the doctor pulled Patty and Jack aside. "Patty, we don't have to tell you that your grandfather is in pain and suffering a great deal. He is also a very strong-willed man. We are in agreement that, without a doubt, he has the strongest will to live off any patient we have ever treated. We also know how much he loves you. I need to ask you to do something for us but, more importantly, for him. Will you be willing to"…

"NO! NO, I won't". She started crying. Heaving sobs that she couldn't contain and didn't try to. "NO, NO, NO, NO, I will not! I knew you were going to ask me to do that! She gasped; you want me to give him permission to just give up the ghost and die. I read things; I know what you are going to ask me." She hugged Jack and cried harder, wailing, not caring at all who heard her. A few people in the hall shed tears, not knowing what was going on, just knowing someone was grieving from the bottom of their hearts. The doctor said not a word. He knew for now it was time to leave it alone.

The following week, Grandpa surprised just about no one. It was time to leave the hospital and go back home. Not to an extended care facility, not to live with a constant care provider that he didn't know. No, he wanted to go home. Patty was fully aware of why he needed that and immediately agreed to stay with him around the clock. She would get a sabbatical from her job if need be. Jack wisely agreed with everything she said and nodded in complete support. His eyes displayed an altogether different message.

Preparation for the transition was relatively simple. A nurse would come by every day to take care of the needful, such as checking his overall condition, feeding him and bathing him. In truth, at this point, the hospital could not do anything more than could be done at home. An emergency signal was installed; always at the ready should Patty have a need for it. The ambulance brought him home with little to no fanfare, just like he wanted.

The first month went well. The transition was a fairly smooth one. Patty and her grandpa talked about everything; he genuinely laughed every day. He would tire easily and fall asleep. It was when he was asleep that the pain demons would arrive. The moaning became more pronounced and louder. He would sound delirious. He would wake up and remember none of it. Jack, of course, had to stay home and take care of things while his wife was away. He did go by daily to see the old man and check on Patty. He couldn't help but notice the strain on her face.

Jack met with Harry once a week to discuss the preparations needed for the transformation of his lawn. It was odd how, when they first started talking about the lawn, he was genuinely excited about it. Now, he was mostly distracted and distant, always wanting to change the subject.

Patty opened Grandpa's window as she had every morning. It was early spring, and the daffodils were already opening. It wouldn't be long before the robins would be proudly strolling around with their heads held high. The fresh air smelled good; spring air always smelled the best, bringing with it fragrances of new beginnings.

She inhaled deeply to take it all in. Grandpa was still asleep, and she hoped he would stay that way for a little longer. Last night had been rough. He woke her up with his groans; he had even cried a little. Grandpa crying. There was a time not so long ago that would have been unimaginable. She got out his favorite album of Red Foley, placed it on the record player and turned the volume down.

He loved the smooth, soothing way Red sang. Years ago, she always objected when he played it because it was so old-fashioned. In truth, she liked Red too. She sat there with him, alone with her thoughts. She wearily let the jumble of emotions, scenarios and inevitable decisions torment her mind.

Things were not improving. Indeed, his situation was getting worse, and the current path they were on was not sustainable. A car turning into the driveway mentally shook her back into the room. It was Jack. He had been so good through all of this. She was genuinely glad to see him. She opened the front door to let him in, kissing him and then kissing him again. There was little need for small talk.

"How is he doing, Patty?" "He slept some last night. He cried most of the night." "Oh wow. Don't think I have ever seen him cry. Didn't think he knew how. Did you talk with the nurse about starting a morphine drip?" "No, not yet. You know him; he is not going to be pleased. You know how hard-headed he can be when his mind is made up. "Look, I know. I just think he will change his mind after the procedure starts. You know he will feel so much better. There really is no reason that he should suffer like this. "If it helps, let me arrange to start the morphine. You have too much on your plate already." "You don't mind? That would help. If Grandpa knew I arranged this, it would hurt him."

Jack stopped her. "If he thought I did it, well, he never liked me that much anyway." "He did too. You just were never good enough for me," she said with a laugh. I will still have to sign off on it since I am his legal guardian." "Then it's settled, let me handle it. A friend of mine might be able to help with the ramifications, legal and otherwise, as well as various other essential things. I'll put a call into her." Jack then kissed the old man on the cheek, then kissed Patty on the cheek and headed for the door.

The procedure was scheduled for the upcoming Friday, the thirteenth of the month. Jack was tied up at work and couldn't be there. The nurse arrived exactly on time. She spoke very little and was a little older than Patty had envisioned. Having said that, she was all business and had an air of confidence about her that put her at ease. She explained to Patty that her grandpa would have to be awake during the procedure to ensure that all was going as planned. She was fully aware of his reluctance to have this done and assured her that everything would be completed out of his field of vision.

She began, "OK, let's get started. Go ahead, and let's wake him up. "Grandpa, the nurse is here to give you a check-up. It shouldn't take long. She told me she was going to have you drink something to clear your throat and stomach, then take a few x-rays; she lied. This won't take long. As Patty was talking, the nurse busied herself preparing everything. She poured him a cup of the solution and had him drink it. She then busied herself with the task at hand. "Let's give the solution a little time to clear his stomach, and we will begin." She was arranging tubes, an apparatus of sorts as if setting up everything for the morphine drip. She asked Patty to bring her some ice water and a few clean cloths. As soon as Patty had left the room, the nurse collected all her things, stuffed them in her medical bag and walked out the front door. Patty never saw her again.

After she left, Jack pulled into the driveway. This had to be handled delicately. Under his breath, he silently said, "Thank you, Clara." Patty, completely confused, finally spoke. "Jack, what happened to the nurse? She just collected her things and walked out. What in the hell is going on?" He put his arms around her and pulled her close. "Patty, let's go check on Grandpa; let's see how he is doing."

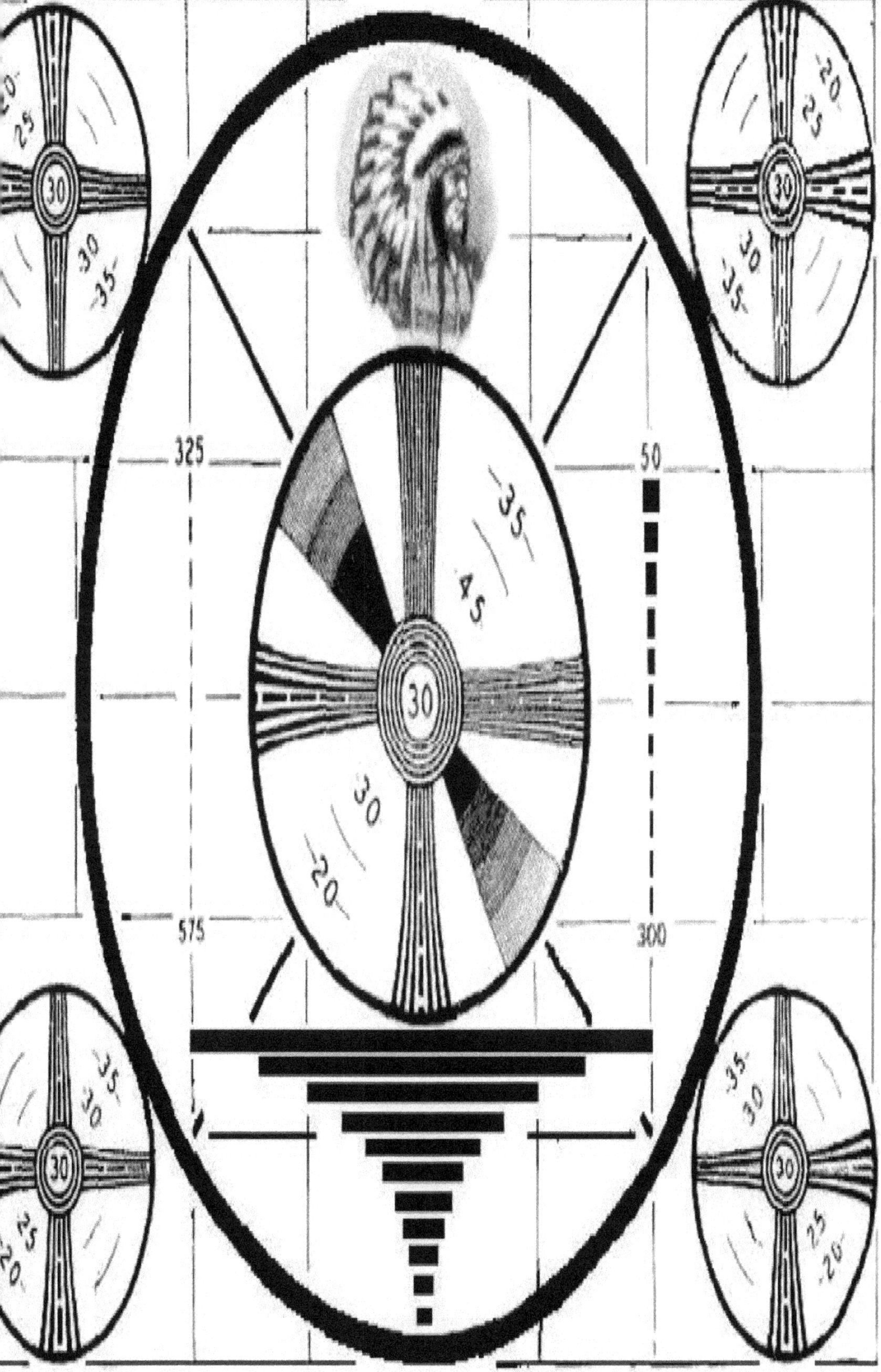

325
575
50
300
35
45
30
20
30
30
30
30
30
30
30
30
25
20
35
35
25
20
35
30
25
20
35
30

FOR NOTES